JBR

JBR is a non-binary creative. He began his career in the 1980s as a child performer with English National Opera, and has spent more than three decades in the industry, exploring creativity and working across a number of fields. He has been an actor, a director, a writer, a designer, a drag queen, a producer, a dramaturg, a teacher, a comedy booker, a publican, a marketing manager and an agent. He started as an agent at Simon & How before setting up on his own as JBR Creative Management, where he works with a small group of brilliant, multi-platform creatives who keep him on his toes, keep him inspired, and keep him learning about the power of creativity.

He holds degrees from Bristol University and Mountview, and a PGCE from London Metropolitan. As a writer, he was contributing editor of *First Act* newspaper, and editor of *Fourthwall Magazine & The Drama Student*. He has contributed to the *Irish Independent, Musical Stages, PostScript*, BritishTheatre.com, and is a columnist for AussieTheatre.com.au. He is often called upon as a judge and has judged film festivals, sat on the Olivier Awards public panel, judged the Amateur Stages playwriting competition, the Stiles + Drewe Mentorship Award, and the New UK Musicals singing competition. He is a regular guest lecturer at a number of UK drama schools.

THE COMPACT GUIDES

are pocket-sized introductions for actors and theatremakers, each tackling a key topic in a clear and comprehensive way. Written by industry professionals with extensive hands-on experience of their subject, they provide you with maximum information in minimum time.

Published – or upcoming – titles include:

BREAKING DOWN YOUR SCRIPT
Laura Wayth

GETTING INTO DRAMA SCHOOL
Nick Moseley

**GETTING, KEEPING & WORKING
WITH YOUR ACTING AGENT**
JBR

**IMPROVING & MAINTAINING
YOUR EMOTIONAL HEALTH**
Andy Barker, Brian Cooley & Beth Wood

LEARNING YOUR LINES
Mark Channon

MAKING SOLO SHOWS
Lisa Carroll & Milly Thomas

**MASTERING A GENERAL
AMERICAN ACCENT**
Rebecca Gausnell

The publisher welcomes suggestions
for future titles in the series.

GETTING, KEEPING & WORKING WITH YOUR ACTING AGENT:

THE COMPACT GUIDE

JBR

NICK HERN BOOKS
London
www.nickhernbooks.co.uk

A Nick Hern Book

Getting, Keeping & Working With Your Acting Agent: The Compact Guide
first published in Great Britain in 2021
by Nick Hern Books Limited, The Glasshouse,
49a Goldhawk Road, London W12 8QP

Designed and typeset by Nick Hern Books, London
Printed and bound in the UK by
Mimeo Ltd, Huntingdon, Cambridgeshire PE29 6XX

A CIP catalogue record for this book
is available from the British Library

ISBN 978 1 84842 941 3

For Rhys

Contents

Introduction

The most essential point I should make at the beginning of this book is that this is not a book about 'Being An Actor'. It is not a book that explains how to be a good actor. It is not a book about how to find work as an actor, nor how to persuade yourself (let alone those around you) that you *are* an actor.

This is a book that discusses how some agents – and some actor–agent relationships – work, and suggests some possible best-practice ideas, whether you are already in a relationship with an agent, hope to start a relationship with an agent, or are struggling to have a productive working relationship with an agent.

This book will *not* act as a categoric, indisputable or unarguable definition of the actor–agent relationship: you will find no definitive list of Dos and Don'ts. Despite the title, you will find no checklist of things you must do in order to get an agent, keep an agent or work with an agent. If you were hoping for such a book, I am afraid I must disabuse you of that thought immediately.

There is no definitive guide. The industry is contradictory and so, by extension, you may find this book contradictory. It will dictate you do one thing and then suggest you do the polar opposite because that is how the industry works. This book will advise you on how some agents work, but will also remind you that not all agents work in the same way. It will address how to market yourself, develop your personal brand and use tried-and-tested techniques to attempt to replicate the success of others, whilst at the same time encouraging you to be individual, stand out from the crowd, and forge your own unique path.

What follows are my thoughts on how I, as an agent, like to work with creatives. This is what I've learned about being a creative – a happy creative at that – through my work as an agent. Advice is only worth what you paid to hear it. I hope you find something here that justifies the scant change from a tenner you've been left with.

The modern acting industry has operated in a relatively similar way for many years and you may find some of this book defaults to an 'If it ain't broke, why fix it?' attitude. Be assured that when I explain how something has worked in the past I am not necessarily arguing that this is the only way it *can* work, or even that it is the best way it might.

I do, however, firmly believe that understanding how the industry has worked in the past, and how some parts of it still work, may provide some benefit to you not only for the here and now, but also for the changes to come.

Can the industry be changed? Yes. Be warned, however, that change rarely involves getting through the doors of the establishment and dismantling from the inside. It is easier to maintain the status quo once inside, to understand the routines, rhythms and structures, and to then write books about how to uphold that structure. It is, in my opinion, far better to dismantle those structures from the outside. To 'blow the bloody doors off' and rebuild. If I write 'this is how it is done', it is not a vindication, nor a recommendation. It is knowledge.

Knowledge is power. Understanding how things work is the first step towards dismantling the structure and rebuilding. Change is coming, there can be no doubt about that. Our creaky, cobwebbed, barely-fit-for-purpose industry is very slowly being dismantled and rebuilt. I ask you to consider imaginative solutions as to how this rebuilding might take place. I ask you too to think about what you want to see in a modern industry: how it looks, what stories we tell, how we represent, how we include, how we adapt to a changing world and a changing industry. Most of all, though, I ask you to think about what kind of careers you may want to build in that industry, who you want to work with, and what matters to you.

I've been fortunate enough to have met, interviewed or worked with some of the people I admire most in this industry, and I have learned there are any number of different routes to follow, and that what is absolutely true for one actor and their journey is completely untrue for another. If my advice connects with you, take it, use it, and see if it works. If it doesn't, if it is at odds with your own experiences, then by all means put it away. What does not seem right for you now, may in time come to be right. Put me on a shelf and dust me off later, I won't mind.

Who Am I?

When I became an agent, my friend the actor Con O'Neill told me, 'Be an agent who loves actors and hates The Industry.' Hate is a strong word but 'The Industry' can certainly frustrate me. Over more than thirty years I've sat in almost every seat on every side of every table. It has been an eclectic career to say the very least. Nonetheless, it's given me a breadth of knowledge and it's given me *opinions*. Sometimes very strong ones.

In *Men Are from Mars, Women Are from Venus*, John Gray wrote:

> To offer a man unsolicited advice is to presume that he
> doesn't know what to do or that he can't do it on his own.

Let me hope that, if you're reading this, you agree that you're soliciting my opinion. I have shared these opinions whenever I'm teaching, lecturing, coaching or working with a client. I share my opinions frequently on social media. I've learned these opinions have helped some people. I've seen fantastic results from people who have taken these opinions and bent them to suit their own personal need. I've seen terrific results from people who already know all this but just needed to hear it again, or hear it at the right time. I've seen people reignite their passion for this industry simply by using these ideas to change their focus. I have also had people disagree, sometimes vehemently, with my opinions.

What do I know about it anyway? I was born in Archway in 1973. My parents emigrated to London from the Republic of Ireland some time in the late 1950s. My mother had been a model, one of Ireland's Pretty Polly girls, and my father hoped to pursue a career as a singer.

A trawl through my family scrapbook reveals pictures of Mum and Dad, stylish and sophisticated; arms draped round Diana Dors; laughing with Morecambe and Wise; Mum sharing a joke with Danny La Rue; Dad in a ruffled shirt coming out of Annabel's nightclub. Dad was a regular on the working-men's-club circuit and was often described in reviews as 'Ireland's answer to Tom Jones'.

Perhaps there was a time when Dad might have 'made it' or broken through, but by the time I, their third child, was born, those scrapbook pictures of the attractive young couple were distant memories. Dad continued on the pub circuit until I was 11 years old and his agent, Alan, was a regular guest for Sunday lunch. I would listen enraptured to Alan's showbiz stories. He was a gregarious, cigar-chomping, Scotch-drinking caricature – all grease and ersatz charm – but he was personable, and he and Dad clearly enjoyed each other's company. Alan was a trusted friend as well as an agent. I guess that was my first lesson in agenting.

At that impressionable age I didn't want to grow up to become Alan. There's a lovely quote that is occasionally – apocryphally – attributed to Dame Maggie Smith: 'No one grows up wanting to be an agent.' Quite right. I didn't want to be Alan, but I did want to be part of his world.

For most of us working in this industry I think it's true that we are first attracted to working in it because we want to be part of a world that appears, at first glance, to be inclusive and accepting – a place where outsiders feel valued. In this world, many of us feel we have found a home, a tribe, a place where we are seen and heard. We are drawn to it. For almost all of us, performing is the entry point into that world. As it was for me.

I played a wise-cracking shepherd in my school Nativity play at 6. I performed a one-man magic show at the school talent assembly at 7. My sister joined the Tricycle Youth Theatre in Kilburn when I was 8 and, when saddled with babysitting duties on a Saturday whilst Mum and Dad did the weekly shop on the Kilburn High Road, she would plonk me in the stalls where I would watch her and her friends rehearse all day.

I wrote my first play at 9. My grandmother made the costumes, I rehearsed my classmates after school and produced it in the school hall. I mashed-up *Les Misérables* with the Nativity story for my family at Christmas at 10;

and, when I was 11, I joined my secondary school choir and we were given the opportunity to sing as part of the backstage chorus in English National Opera's *Parsifal* at the London Coliseum.

The following year I made my on-stage debut at the Coliseum. I spent the next seven years growing up backstage at English National Opera, playing many of opera's leading boy roles. Meanwhile, at school we lacked a drama department so I started a drama group and directed and produced a play in the dining hall. At 18 I was cast in my first adult role at ENO and for my first term at Bristol University, where I was studying Film, Television & Drama, I travelled back and forth to London three times a week to play the part.

At Bristol I produced, acted, directed, designed and drank. On graduating I returned to London to pursue the lights of the West End. I signed with an agent fairly quickly and worked the stage door of the Dominion for several years. Eventually I quit and took a 'real job' in marketing for a beer company. In the evenings I worked the cabaret circuit just as my dad had. I worked as a drag queen, comedy booker and cabaret agent before I finally trained as a teacher and taught Drama at a secondary school. I was suited and booted for teaching by day, but by night I continued to haul my heels and wigs around London's gay bars. After a couple of years I retrained in musical theatre at Mountview and, after graduating, spent seven years pursuing my dream, growing increasingly unhappy, until the writer Stephen Beresford asked me to read for the small role of a drag queen in his first feature film, *Pride*.

Stephen remembered seeing my drag act sixteen years earlier and we'd kept in touch, so he knew I was still performing. Whilst working on *Pride*, Stephen introduced me to a number of people in TV production and agenting, and for the first time in three decades I became more interested in what else I could do with my life rather than pursuing an acting career. I knew it was time to move on, and by the time *Pride* was released, I was working as an agent with a small list of actors.

I grew up in a time when Equity was stronger. I've seen many changes. I've been working in this industry for more than thirty years and it has become literally my entire life. It is an obsession that grows with each passing year. I am surprised by the speed of some changes, frustrated by the time it takes for others.

More than anything, though, I have not forgotten the many, many years of stomach-clenching doubt; of waiting for the phone to ring, of loneliness and feeling like I was missing out. For the best part of the last decade I've been an agent and found it has utilised my various skills and interests in a way I never thought possible. I didn't grow up wanting to be an agent, but I'm certainly delighted it is what I've become.

Agenting is one of the many great mysteries of our industry. There's a lack of clarity as to what agents do, how the relationship with their clients works, what their influence is, what their contracts mean. I find it confusing and obfuscating, and when I think back to my years as an actor, I wish I'd known then what I know now about agents. In short, I wish I'd had this book.

What Does an Agent Do?

I am often asked in interviews: 'What does an agent do?' Personally, I think a far more interesting question is: 'Why do agents do it?' – but I will come to that.

Once upon a time, not so long ago, actors didn't need agents. In an interview for *Fourthwall Magazine*, Penelope Keith, in her seventies at the time, had a few choice words to say about agents:

> We never thought about agents in my day. I don't remember anyone at Webber Douglas, ever, talking about being rich or famous, or wanting to be a star. It didn't enter our heads. You wanted to work and you wanted to learn. And that is very, very different now… And what do agents know? Truly? What do they know? They know what they can cast and get some money with for a year, there is no career progression, no one takes care of your career.

This is something you may hear rather a lot from a certain generation of actors – yes, they have agents, but many consider them to be a necessary evil, someone who helps them run their business rather than someone who manages their career for them.

It is true that in recent years 'getting an agent' has become something of an obsession. Goodness, someone has probably even written a book on how to do it! It has become, for many drama schools, something of a marker of how successful they are. You will often see schools using '100% of graduates have been signed by agents' as part of their marketing.

Many schools have an Industry Liaison Officer – a member of staff whose job it is to get agents to attend shows and showcases, to foster good relationships between the school and the industry, and, in part, to help students get signed. Whether it actually does the students any good to indulge this obsession with getting an agent is debatable. It encourages the belief that *any* agent is better than no agent.

Quite simply, that is not the case. Agents are great, many agents are incredible, most are lovely people, the vast majority of agents truly care about their clients and about the industry they work in – but it's true too that many do not. Many are, as Penelope Keith implied, interested only in making money. An agency is, after all, a business. Agents make their money from their clients, but not all agents contribute to the industry, or even prove their value to the client.

As with people in any business, there are good agents and there are bad agents. Far better for drama schools to teach graduates how to manage their own careers than to fob them off on any old agent just so they can boast of a hundred per cent record.

There are many different types of agents. Some call themselves 'personal managers', some 'boutique'. Some work for huge companies, some for small. Some work mainly in commercials, some in theatre, some in film. Most will work across all media, whilst some may have particular specialities. Of vital importance is working out what type of agent you want and need, and recognising that your need may change as your career progresses.

It is simply incorrect to instil the belief that any agent is better than no agent. An agent should be tailored to your specific needs, wants and interests. Most actors will move through a few agents in their careers. Landing the perfect first agent is not actually that important, but getting the wrong agent at the beginning of your career can be detrimental.

There are very many things that modern agents do, and the role has changed over time. One of the things agents do is find people jobs. That is often considered to be the primary role of an agent. An agent is there to make your life easier, to handle the contracts, to negotiate the deal, to ensure that you are fairly looked after, represented and taken care of. These are often the things that clients are not particularly good at. Creatives are, on the whole, not always sure exactly how to sell themselves.

An agent's primary job is to look after their clients – to *represent* them. Some people advocate that an agent works *for* you, some say you work together. A good analogy is to imagine you are both working on the railways; you will be driving the train, but your agent is out in front, laying down the tracks. If you're not communicating effectively about what direction you're both going in, then this train is going to crash.

The finding of work is just one of the roles of an agent. Billy Porter, in a Masterclass interview for Carnegie Mellon in 2013, said it best when he said:

> Your agent takes ten per cent. Don't ever expect them to do more than ten per cent of the work. And so they do ten per cent of the work. So the moment that you think that you're about to have an attitude with your agent, look at yourself, and make sure that you're doing your ninety per cent.

In an increasingly competitive marketplace, actors need to be out there looking for work themselves, creating their own work, working with other creatives, and building their own network. An agent's job is to negotiate the contracts, and deal with all the technical and business stuff of the industry that creatives are often not interested in or don't know too much about. The best resource an agent has is their clients. The information that comes into the office from clients is invaluable.

There are certain misconceptions about agenting, certain ideas that are either more to do with the American style of agenting, or are left over from a time when there were fewer agents and fewer actors. It is more rare than you'd think that a UK casting director of a major feature film would ring up one agent to book in a big star, and ask the agent to fill in all the smaller roles from their new signings or new graduates on their books.

American agents tend to be involved more in the 'packaging' of projects than we are in the United Kingdom. Packaging a project will often involve an agency like CAA or William Morris Endeavour building an entire project from scriptwriter to director to main star and selling the entire package to a film studio. In these instances, yes, it is in the interest of the big agencies to include roles for their smaller clients. However, the UK has never really taken to packaging as a concept. Agencies over here are less involved with packaging entire deals, and many agents are understandably wary about allowing their clients to work on a film production that is being completely managed by a single other agency.

The UK's main casting platform is Spotlight, where casting directors are able to upload the casting breakdowns and briefs for their projects. This has seen greater transparency in the industry with less reliance on who one knows, and has led to a proliferation of new agencies springing up.

As with any industry, regulation can be a problem. The Personal Managers' Association (PMA) can be a very good resource to see if an agency has agreed to be bound by their suggested list of best-practice guidelines for the industry. But whilst their members all agree to a certain set of guidelines, the PMA is not a regulatory body. The world of agenting can be a bit like the Wild West. It can be difficult to know who has your back, who doesn't, who has fair business practices, and which practices might be exploitative.

It is important to understand how an agency works financially. An agent works for you without compensation until you start making money. It can take a new signing about eight to twelve months before they begin to book jobs and start earning, so there is a period at the beginning where agents are working for you, promoting you, talking you up, and trying to get you seen, without being paid.

An individual actor would have to be earning an awful lot of money to be the one actor who covers an agent's complete salary. It is the *collective* commission from all clients that pay an agent's salary. That collective commission also pays the overheads for the office, the assistant's salary, gifts and all expenses, including travel and theatre tickets.

When you're out of work, your agent is still working for you; it's not in their interests to stop. They are still doing what they do; always looking for the chance to maximise your work opportunities. An agent will submit you for hundreds of jobs that you never even get to hear about. They make decisions about you every day that you have no control over. That's why, when thinking about what an agent does, it is important to realise that for them to do their job well, you have to play your part too.

This is why you have to have a relationship with your agent, to be able to talk to them in the good times and the bad times. They believe in you, they mentor you, they nurture your career, they try to inspire you and they commiserate with you. Agents are there for a thousand things that are beyond any job description of what an agent does. They advise clients on moving house, they give references to letting agencies, they write recommendations for 'real-world' jobs, they sometimes even feed their clients. Agents try to remember birthdays and try to be there during important life events. An agent is so much more than just the day-to-day office work of your career. An agent is one half of a relationship.

Agencies earn money from commission on your fee, taking a percentage of your earnings. Most agents will take somewhere between ten and fifteen per cent, although some take twenty per cent or more. Most have a sliding scale for TV, film and theatre work, so you pay slightly less on theatre work than you do on TV and film, and you'll pay slightly more on commercials. The longer you're with an agent and the more money you are bringing in, the more power you have and the more you can negotiate your commission. There are some top agents with star clients who set their commission levels at eight per cent across the board, and many agents take a lower commission on repeating jobs, so if you stay in a long-running stage or TV show for more than a year, some agents will take a lower commission on the extended years.

Some production companies will pay your agent a twenty per cent fee, known as an 'agency fee', in addition to your agreed fee. If it is the practice of your agency to accept an agency fee it should be clearly laid out in your original contract with them. The agency fee will be on top of your agreed fee so your agent will take that twenty per cent, *and* they will take their commission from you.

So much for what an agent *does*. But the more interesting question is: *why* do they do it?

Many agents are former performers. They have had their careers in the performing arts and have decided, for whatever reason, to move to 'the other side'. Perhaps they just got older, perhaps their knees don't allow them to dance quite as much as they used to, maybe too many cigarettes prevent them from singing as high, or as fast or as purely as they once did. Maybe they tired of the endless rounds of auditions, of never hearing back. Maybe their self-esteem took one too many knocks. Some agents may have trained in performing arts and realised early on that their interests or particular skill set lends themselves more to encouraging others, developing other people's talents. Performing is a hard-knock life and even the most bright-eyed, bushy-tailed and ambitious may decide it is not for them.

Some are drawn to agenting because they think they can make decent money out of it. They may want to be part of the industry but have no desire to be on stage. There are as many different reasons for becoming an agent as there are different reasons for becoming a performer. A good agent will want to know why you are interested in a career in performing arts, and it's probably very interesting for you to ask your prospective agent why they were interested in working in this industry in the first place, and what keeps them doing it.

The answer to the question 'Why?' may give you an idea of any particular speciality or area of interest. Like most performers, most agents want to work across all fields. However, there may be agents who are more drawn towards working in theatre, or musical theatre, or TV or film. They may be passionate about different film directors' styles and genres, or have a particular interest in audio drama. It may be that finding out your prospective agent's particular area of interest can help you to make a decision about whether they are the right agent for you, whether they have the right knowledge and contacts to guide and help you to develop your career in all the areas and fields that you want to work in.

None of this is to say that an agent who is particularly skilled or interested in musical theatre cannot also be a great TV and film agent. Dealing with contracts is essentially the same regardless of whether it's for TV, film, musical theatre, theatre, audio drama, commercials or whatever else. However, you might find that an agent who began their career in musical theatre and has a particular interest in that field may be able to advise you better on singing teachers, dance teachers and how to keep your skill set fresh than one who did not. They will certainly know the particular demands of that field, which may be important to you.

Overall, an agent is there to represent. They are your voice in the industry. They represent you to the industry; therefore it is important that they represent the industry that you want to see. It is important that the voice of the person you choose to represent you is representing you in the way that you wish to be represented. For me, that means fairness and equity in representation and diversity, ensuring that people from all backgrounds and all voices, races, genders, sexualities, sizes, shapes and abilities are represented and given the same opportunities.

Types of Agencies

Broadly speaking, agencies can be divided into big, mid-size, small, boutique, personal management and cooperative agencies.

Big agencies boast a roster of clients that will include household names. Huge conglomerate agencies are often international and deal with 'star' clients. For some actors, signing with a huge agency is the Holy Grail. It is pretty cool to be signed by one of the top agencies and receive that validation and feel-good factor. It can provide a much-needed confidence boost and, in some cases, catapult a career into the stratosphere. An agency thrives on information and the bigger the client, the better the information. If your agent is dealing with A-list talent then they are talking to A-list producers and A-list casting directors – so it stands to reason they are getting A-list information.

Most mid-sized, small and boutique agencies are all getting roughly the same information, but the really big agencies are hearing about projects years and years in advance. Reading an early draft of a blockbuster film script is very different to reading a casting director's interpretation of that script a little further down the line. Knowing who is attached to a project in its early stages, who is financing it, what the budget is: all of this is incredibly valuable information. Whether that filters directly down to the new signing is debatable.

All agents make their money from commission and the commission for an A-list artist on an A-list project is a lot of money. Equity minimum commission is not so much. Huge agencies have huge overheads. They have a lot of office space, they have a lot of agents, they have a lot of expenses to cover, therefore, as a business, it makes sense that a priority needs to be a focus on A-list talent and securing a high fee. That's just good business.

If you've been signed by a big agency then you should know they are signing you because they are investing in you and want to get you to that A-list level. The bigger the agent, the busier they are, so finding out how they intend to develop your career is important.

You may be spending most of your time talking to an assistant and rarely speak to the agent who originally signed you. How important is it to have a relationship with your agent? There's an old saying that no actor wants to be a star, but every agent wants to sign one. You have to think about whether that's the path you want to take, whether the path of fame and fortune and becoming an internationally famous movie star is really what you want. Weigh up the pros and cons of this. Getting what you want can sometimes be the worst thing in the world, particularly if you get it before you're ready.

There is so much scrutiny of A-list stars these days, how we focus on them, how we interrogate and dissect every single thing they say. You may not be ready for this. It may not be the path you want to take. Do you want to be flying all over the world and never settling in one place, or do you want to work in community theatre, do you want to go back to the region you came from and encourage young people? Communicating your desires to your agent is so important. Knowing who you are, what you're doing, and why you are doing it is vital.

Remember, of course, that the commission your agent is going to get on a huge film is much more than the commission they're going to get on a small theatre job, and so your agent may be more inclined to develop a big career for you. But what if you see your career as being more in theatre than in TV and film? What if you don't like TV and film? Believe it or not, lots of people actually don't like the hours and hours of hanging around on set and getting up early in the mornings! What if your work is going to be primarily in theatre? You may feel that your work is not valued as much as somebody who is bringing in huge amounts of commission. Do you want personal attention, do you want to feel in control of your career, do you want to be a small fish in a very big pond? These are all things to consider.

It's very exciting to get an offer from a big agency, but you should also think about whether it is the career path you want to take. Do you want to be dealing with the second assistant, rather than the agent? The talent is the power, but there is a lot to be said for being with an agent who is themselves a big talent. There are lots of agents in the industry who are themselves very well known in their own right. With that kind of power comes a lot of information. It can be hugely beneficial to your career to be with that type of agent.

Developing and nurturing talent is important as well. When you're hot and you're bringing in a lot of information and a lot of commission, you are part of the infrastructure – you are literally paying your way. What happens when you're not? When you're not bringing in the money? It can be very exciting to be straight out of school and signed by a big agency. There's a huge advantage to building a long relationship with your agent so, of course, there's a big advantage to spotting talent in the early stages and signing them. But not everyone's career moves at a predictable pace. What happens if something happens in your life that takes your focus away from your career? Will that agent still be there for you?

A mid-size agency may be mid-size because it is comfortable being mid-size, or because it is on its way to becoming a bigger agency. It is always really useful to ask a mid-size agent what their ambitions are. Do they want to become a huge conglomerate agency? Does their ambition, as an agency, lie with nurturing talent and building long relationships with them, or is their ambition and energy going into becoming a big agency?

A mid-size agency will often have a good balance of agents and assistants, and you may feel that you are getting better personal attention from your team. It is likely that the spread of talent and work at a mid-size agency means that, instead of a large number of A-list clients taking your agent's time and attention away from you, there may be only a handful of big clients. With fewer overheads there is usually less need to make big money quickly. A smaller client list may mean considerably more personal attention and a more individual approach to your career. You may have heard the mantra that a mid-size, or smaller, agency works harder because they have to. There is a certain element of truth to that, but the pay-off might be having an agent who is working super-hard for fifty other clients as opposed to an agent who has assistants they can spread the workload across.

'Boutique' is a word that, in the last few years, has come to be a synonym for small. However, what boutique really means is 'specialised'. A traditional boutique agency is an agency that has a speciality in some field so they may be a boutique dance agency, or a boutique commercial agency, or a boutique voice-over agency. If they truly are a boutique agency, then make sure they are specialised in the area you want to work in. For many performers a true boutique agency that specialises in a particular area is far more attractive than any other agency. You'll know that all the work you are being suggested for is something you are truly interested in and want to do. You'll know that your agent considers themselves an expert in the area, so will be on hand to share their years of knowledge and experience with you. You'll know, with a true boutique agency, that you're getting exactly what it says on the tin.

A further type of agency you may come across is the personal management company. We work with personal managers in the UK far less than in the United States, where many actors have both an agent *and* a manager, and pay commission to both. There are certain agencies in the UK that call themselves personal management companies but, like 'boutique', the term has frequently come to be used as another synonym for small. A personal manager should offer you a directly personal experience, uniquely tailored to you and your career, and provide a level of personal attention that goes above and beyond the usual actor–agent relationship. A personal manager will usually work with a relatively small number of clients and their aim is to provide a bespoke service for each individual client, overseeing and nurturing a fruitful and longstanding relationship.

Finally, a wonderful type of agency are cooperative agencies, where all the people working in the agency are usually working actors themselves and share the workload. A cooperative is a terrific introduction to the business side of agenting. During your working days in the office you will gain insight into the entire process of agenting: how breakdowns are written, how jobs are cast, how auditions operate, and how the business of running an agency works.

Understanding the business side of acting is very useful for anybody in the industry, and being part of a team working towards a common purpose can be very inspiring. However, the downsides of a cooperative may be not having one particular person responsible for your career, and with a number of different people and personalities working in the office on any given day, there may be a different set of priorities.

Ultimately, it comes down to the relationship you want with an agent, knowing what you want from your career, finding an agent that wants the same things, and knowing that you can talk to them about it. Perhaps the most important agent, the one you will have the longest relationship with, and the one whose opinion is most valuable to you is –

You.

You are your own best agent. Being as involved in your own career as you possibly can is so important because you are the best agent for you. Agents are salespeople. They sell their clients. Whether you know it or not, you are better at selling yourself than anybody else is. You know yourself back to front. If you are constantly learning and developing, finding out what you like and what you don't like, if you are constantly interrogating your own skill set and your own interests, then you will know yourself better than any other agent could possibly know you. Learn to develop a critical eye for your work, for your CV, for your headshot, and how you're packaging and selling yourself.

Do you *need* an agent? The answer is no. You absolutely do not. The role of an agent is a relatively new addition to the industry and a fairly modern way of working. Once upon a time, you would come out of drama school and, as Penelope Keith said, you would simply want a job, any job at all.

An agent is there to represent you and to advise you. It is perfectly possible to represent yourself. Indeed, many actors do this very successfully. Whilst there are advantages to having an agent – having somebody to ring up, moan at, talk to, work through problems with, ask for advice, have as a friend, a sounding board, and a mentor all rolled into one – there is absolutely no reason why you should not be able to do all this for yourself. Being self-represented is a scary decision to make, but there is no shame in it. In fact, many successful performers are self-represented, and don't rely on an agent either to find them work or to manage their careers for them. It is, as everything, an option. Your journey is your journey.

1. Getting...

Getting an agent is often seen as an obstacle that needs to be overcome, or the first step on the way to becoming a working actor. It is neither. An agent is simply something one may choose to acquire along the route, someone to walk the path with you whilst you acquire other skills and build your CV.

Getting an agent is not the end point, nor is it the point at which the real work of becoming an actor starts. Like everything, like learning to act itself, getting an agent is a process. Understanding that process will make acquiring an agent easier, and will help you to understand more about what agents are looking for and how to present yourself to them, and will even teach you a little about how the business side of the industry works.

Who Are You?

The single piece of advice that will serve you best, not just at the beginning of your career but throughout, is 'Be yourself.'

This advice is going to come at you from everyone you speak to. Acting coaches will tell you, agents will beg you, casting directors will say it is all they are looking for. You will tweet it, post it on Instagram, pin it to your mood boards. There are any number of different inspirational quotes that will be liked, shared or retweeted, from the lofty 'γνῶθι σεαυτόν' ('Know thyself'), as inscribed on the Oracle at Delphi, to the camp 'Know who you are and deliver at all times', preached by RuPaul.

Knowing yourself is where we'll begin. Not with how to write an email, not with who to approach, not with how to sell yourself. You may, of course, leap forward to those chapters and plough straight ahead with sending a thousand applications for representation to every agent listed in Contacts – but it will be a waste of time.

Begin at the beginning. Start with working out who you are and what makes you different to the seventy thousand other actors listed on Spotlight. Knowing *why* you stand out and *what* makes you unique will make the onerous task of actually standing out and being unique far easier.

It may be distasteful to employ the language of the corporate boardroom in the creative workplace, but actors are a commodity and it is your agent's job to market you. To be basic: an agent sells and a casting director buys, so it's worth spending a little bit of time working out who you are and what you have to offer, to know what it is you've got for sale.

Here's the truth: very often we don't know what we're looking for until we see it. Bold, decisive choices being made by people who know what they can offer are what capture attention in the audition room. The weakest auditions are generally given by those who attempt to predict what the panel are looking for.

Actors who know who they are bring authenticity to their roles because they understand that acting is not 'putting something on' – it is understanding what to reveal. Actors do not 'pretend to be other people'. Children in a playground pretend to be other people. Great actors interpret, filter and distil through their own experiences, skill and technique. Actors are artists, not children playing dress-up. An actor who understands who they are and what they bring to the table will make better and braver choices than an actor who is unsure of themselves. Orson Welles, in the 1995 documentary *Orson Welles: The One-Man Band*, described this philosophy perfectly:

> Acting is like sculpture, it's what you take away from yourself to reveal the truth of what you're doing that makes a performance.

Do you know what your offering is? Do you know what it is you bring to the table? How do you present yourself to the world outwardly? Please take some time to answer the following questions before you hurtle ahead:

- *What is my age range?*
  Be honest and realistic. Stockard Channing may have played a high-schooler in *Grease* when she was 33 (a gap of fifteen years), but your playing age is unlikely to be any more than five years either side of your real age.

- *What is my physical type?*
  Are you stocky/plus-size? Slim? Average? Toned/muscular? Tall/short?

- *What is my voice type?*
  Is your voice rich and deep, or high and light? Do you speak with resonance? Do you command attention when you speak? Do you have a wide range of vocal tones and colours in your everyday speech, or are you more limited? What about pace? Are you slow and thoughtful, or fast and chatty?

- *What energy do I give off? What is my personality?*
  This is quite an important one, but often overlooked. What energy do you bring into the room? Are you

bubbly and light, intimidating or scary? Are you warm and inviting, or stand-offish? Do people warm to you quickly and easily, or are you more reserved? Are you the life and soul of the party or are you a quiet wallflower? Are you outgoing or introverted? Do you love meeting new people and getting involved with a new group, or are you more comfortable around people you know well?

- *Who do I want to be?*
  Sometimes it is useful to frame this question as 'How do I want to be remembered?' What attributes and traits are most important to you? This is not asking who you want to become, it is more about what traits you already have that you are most proud of. What type of person do you want to be? If you had the choice, how would you want people to think of you?

- *Who is my audience?*
  Who do you want to be seen by? Are you more drawn to working in gritty urban dramas, or do you feel affinity with period work? Will a typical audience take to you more in light comedy or in classical drama? A classic Hollywood action hero, or waif-like heroine? Where is an average audience less likely to question you?

- *What is my ideal outcome?*
  Right now, with your current look, personality and skill set, what is your ideal outcome? What is your most likely casting? All actors dream of having a versatile career and most believe they could play anything, given the chance, but it's good to begin with truly understanding your limitations.

- *What is my consistent offering?*
  Who are you in the morning? What is your day-to-day offering to the world? When you're not pretending to be someone else, who are you, most consistently?

- *What is my unique story?*
  No one can be you, the way that you can. The unique circumstances of your birth, upbringing and training have created you. What is the individual, unique story of your life so far?

A keen eye will notice that many of these are not fixed attributes. Physical shape can be changed, muscles can be worked on, weight can be lost or gained, a voice type can be altered, hair can be cut. It is astonishing how many changes can be made. Consider, first, what you have right now. What are you working with at this moment?

This leads on to discussions of stereotyping and questions of representation, of how we are perceived in a visual industry. Pamela Robertson Wojick, in her essay 'Typecasting', published in *Criticism, vol. 45, no. 2* (2003), wrote that 'most actors reject typecasting. Rare indeed is the actor who admits being happily typecast. In fact, film actors have decried typecasting almost since the beginning of film-making.'

Knowing how you are usually perceived is not the same as agreeing to it. It is incumbent upon all of us in the industry to reject outdated tropes and to encourage a more inclusive and diverse industry. We must be wary, in this approach to finding out our 'type', that it does not become an exercise in stereotypes. Type is shared characteristics, typical of 'the ideal' of a group or class, whereas stereotype is a formulaic and simplified conception, usually based on image. In an industry that is highly visual and a screen language that is based in semiotics, we need to walk the fine line of understanding type whilst striving to avoid stereotype. In order to work against type, or to challenge stereotypes, beginning with an investigation of how we are currently perceived will help us to understand where we might place in a visual industry and the existing semiotics of screen.

In the actor–agent relationship, the agent is making decisions every day about the actor – and the actor has little control over it. There are many biases in our industry that we would do well to recognise. We must all work together to challenge the outdated biases that have been accepted, and actors who find themselves repeatedly asked to audition for the same type of character should be prepared to raise this as a concern with their agent. Andrew Scott, speaking to *Fourthwall Magazine,* put it succinctly:

> Once you're in a show that's successful, you can suddenly be asked to do the same thing all of the time. But if you don't want to, you just have to not say yes, you know? It's pretty simple.

The personality types are usually much more interesting to investigate than the physical types – after all, you can change many things about how you look but underneath, pretty much, you remain the same person.

Once you've answered the list of questions above, ask some friends to answer them about you as well. You may be surprised at the answers. You may find it challenging to realise that your friends don't see you in the way you see yourself. Understanding how, and why, others see you in the way they do is all part of the journey of understanding what it is you present to the world, and how the world sees you. Weirdly, one of the best ways to find out more about yourself is to ask other people. We can be unusually ignorant of our own strengths, not to mention peculiarly blind when it comes to our faults. Asking other people how they see you can be painful but also revelatory. It may confirm what you think of yourself or it may contradict it.

Speaking of contradictions, once you've asked other people what they think of you, learn when to ignore it. Other people may have an ulterior motive for their response. Your private tutor might not want to lose you as a client, your loved ones perhaps won't see you quite as dispassionately as you need them to, some of your peers may even be jealous of you. You are also unlikely to get the best results from simply putting your headshot up on social media and asking these questions, as many people will simply agree with what other people have said rather than thinking it through for themselves.

You're probably familiar with the approach to text that asks you to go through a script making a note of what your character says about themselves and what others say about your character, examining how your character is seen on the outside, and contrasting that with how the character sees themselves.

Think of Malvolio in *Twelfth Night*, for example. Much of the humour, and indeed almost all of the pathos, comes from the contrast between how he sees himself and how he is seen by others, what is shown versus what is concealed. This standard acting exercise is a wonderful way to create layers and depth in character. So look at yourself as if you were a character. If the unexamined life is not worth living, you had better get examining.

In exactly the same way as approaching a role by examining the inner and outer characteristics of the character, it is also vitally important that you know your *own* inner and outer characteristics too. The questions you answered above, if answered honestly, will have given you some indication of your 'outers' and 'inners'. Now, just as you would with a character analysis, filter other people's opinions of your outer through what you know about your inner. No one but no one knows or understands you better than you do yourself.

A word of caution when doing this forensic examination of yourself: learn to distinguish fact from interpretation.

- *Fact*: If you are six-foot tall you will never play Boq the Munchkin in a professional production of *Wicked*.

- *Interpretation*: If you are buxom, petite and quirky, you will never play the romantic lead.

Do not confuse irrefutable, unalterable facts with disputable, contentious interpretations.

You may find it difficult to place yourself under the microscope. Most of us do. Doubtless you have been told hundreds of times that you need to develop a thick skin to survive in this industry. Well, you do, and it requires practice. It requires you to be more honest and analytical of yourself than anyone else would ever dare to be.

Use all your acting training and turn it on yourself. Hot-seat yourself, ask yourself difficult and probing questions, interview yourself as though you were Andrew Neil asking the questions, not Ellen DeGeneres. Incorporate the practice of unfiltered stream-of-consciousness writing into your daily routine. Familiarise yourself with and practise the Johari window technique for self-awareness. Try a Myers–Briggs test or look into your Enneagram personality type. All these are available for free on the internet and, if nothing else, can provide an entertaining half-hour. Investigate yourself both dispassionately and with compassion.

In all of this work and analysis, you should bear in mind that where and who you are now is not fixed forever. Check in with yourself regularly. As you grow and develop as an actor, as you experience life and are challenged, you will change. Your 21-year-old self will have a very different outlook on life than your 41-year-old self, or even your 31-year-old self. Knowing who you are right now will also give you a guide as to where you need assistance and nurturing, where you need to develop.

An honest and in-depth understanding of who you currently are will also help you to avoid comparing yourself to others. We all do this. In the age of social media it is almost impossible to avoid doing this, even though we know it's ridiculous. We know that comparing our insides to someone else's outside is pointless. We know we are comparing our first rehearsal to someone else's press night – and yet we continually do it.

Our Instagram, our Twitter feed, our Facebook profiles are not the full story of who we are. They are just the stories we want to present to the world. Social-media accounts only tell part of the story, showing a constructed personality with little nuance or subtlety. What we present is an idealised version of our life. What we see on social media is often very far from the truth. Forget about comparing yourself to someone else. The only way you're going to find your route through the woods is to acknowledge and accept that you are carving out your *own* path.

Some books aimed at actors will talk about the work of 'knowing yourself' as though it's a question of discovering your brand. Branding is a useful marketing exercise that's about building on the perceptions others have of you. A brand is not something you sit down and design from scratch. Determining brand values involves examining not only your own perceptions of yourself, but also analysing what others think or say about you. Your brand is what you present to the world: all the good bits, some of the flaws, neatly packaged up and presented in the most flattering light. Theoretically, your brand might represent what you stand for, who you perceive yourself to be, and the type of actor you want to become.

That said, branding for an actor is balderdash – here's why: Branding identifies a product for sale in a specific market. It is not usually about taking a completely unique product and selling it. It is about looking at the restrictions, traditions and parameters of the existing marketplace and identifying how one particular brand is better than others within those restrictions. Branding relies on every offering within the market sector being approximately the same, but highlighting areas where one brand is a bit better than others.

You are not a brand. You cannot view yourself as completely unique and original if you see yourself as being broadly the same as everyone else. Whilst branding for actors is useful up to a point, it does not leave you room or scope to be unique and individual. It encourages you to be roughly the same as everyone else. Be careful about branding yourself to be the same as everyone else. Do not let branding lead you to ignore a real and truthful investigation into what makes you completely and utterly unique.

When you define your brand with a perceived audience (that casting director whose eye you want to catch, that agent you want to attract) in mind, you are in danger of defining who you are based on outside perspectives. Your brand becomes a fixed story, but our personal stories are fluid and changeable, they are not permanent. The goal with this work is to learn how to express yourself authentically, not to conform to what you perceive the 'market' wants you to be. Authenticity is the aim.

On 'knowing yourself', the actor Jenna Russell probably says it best:

> If I could look back, I would say 'Trust who you are.'
> That's the only thing you've got. You are your unique thing.
> It's going to fit some things and not fit others. Be at peace
> with that. Trust in saying 'This is who I am.'

Do the work. Find out who you are. Tell the world.

Researching Agents

Before you start emailing agents, first you must research them. Having engaged in detailed, extensive work on yourself, finding out who you are and what your consistent offering is, you will have begun to have some thoughts on the type of agent that is right for you at this particular moment. Your research on agents is a continuation of that process. But it is also the area a lot of actors fall down on. Too often they rush it or overlook it, leading them to approach agents who are unsuitable for them or to approach them in the wrong way.

Research is a vitally important skill for actors. Casting directors recommend it as imperative to an actor's preparation, advising actors to thoroughly research the production team, director and writer before coming into the room. Given this is such an important skill, it makes sense that an actor would want to demonstrate their ability to do it. If you do not accurately research the agency you are applying to, then we may, reasonably, assume you will not do research around the auditions we send you up for. Demonstrating your research ability and attention to detail, particularly in a first approach to an agent, should not be underestimated.

An incorrect or badly researched approach is usually a waste of an actor's precious time. A lot of this can be solved if you do the research at the beginning, and work smarter, not harder.

It may be that many actors, whilst taught how to prepare and research a role, are not taught how to use those skills to research agencies.

One of the most valuable ways to research agencies is to use Spotlight. You can research their online database, Contacts, which has a list of all agents working in the industry. A Google search is also useful, or you might download the current members list from the Personal Managers' Association (PMA). *The Actors' and Performers' Yearbook* is very useful, as is IMDb where, if you are a pro-member, you can research actors and see who their agents are. You may also find it helpful to read industry papers like *The Stage* or *Backstage*.

Perhaps the most useful method is to ask around amongst your friends, people that you've worked with, casting directors, directors and contacts in the industry. Use social media too; Twitter lists can be very handy. You'll find that other Twitter users will have created lists of agents in the industry. Subscribing to those lists is a good way of building up a contacts book of agents quickly.

Have a look at an agent's website and see the type of work their clients are doing. Do you recognise it? If their clients are involved in a lot of self-produced work, or a lot of one-person shows, it's unlikely the agent would have had much involvement in that. Be on the lookout for jobs you know could only have come through an agent rather than just looking at the number of credits somebody has.

Investigating the size of the client list might be useful, although not always possible as many agencies do not have a full client list easily available. Is there a perfect number of clients per agent? This is a very difficult question to answer even with a ballpark figure. Somewhere between fifty and one hundred is probably the ideal, but it depends on the agent, on the kind of work their clients are doing, and on the type of agency they are. Very large commercial or dance agencies who work with big block bookings of talent may have considerably more than one hundred clients. The number of clients an agent can effectively represent also depends on whether they have assistants working with them, how long they've been practising in the industry, and how many of their clients are working at any one time. There is no magic number.

As well as the number of clients, ask yourself about their quality. Have you heard of them? Many creatives are impressed by agencies that boast high-calibre clients with names that are familiar to them. Whilst this is undoubtedly a useful thing to look at, your own individual journey in this industry is just that – individual. Comparing yourself to, or emulating the career of, other creatives is unlikely to produce the same results. Consider not only the calibre of clients, but the calibre of work they're doing. People may be very well known in one particular field – musical theatre, for example – but unknown outside of it.

There's nothing wrong with an agency that represents lots of clients you haven't heard of. There are hundreds of thousands of actors in the UK and they all work in different fields and different genres. Some are household names, some are well known in their field, some are terrific jobbing actors who are rarely out of work but whose name may not be recognisable outside of the industry. Just because you haven't heard of them, doesn't mean that they are not a good actor with an enviable career. An agent's list may well include actors of all types, ranging from household names through to emerging talent.

Think about where you currently sit in the industry and who your CV is currently appealing to. This may involve a period of adjusting your expectations. If you are young, and your work so far consists mainly of your drama-school and local theatre productions, the chance of you being signed by United Agents, Independent Talent or any similar agencies that work with huge international talent is very small. It's not impossible, by any means, and a lot of this industry does rely on luck – but it is unlikely. At this point in your career you may well be better off with an agent specialising in new and emerging talent, or one who works particularly with young people. Do be realistic about where you currently sit in the industry.

It can be helpful to organise agencies into categories; perhaps as A*, A, B, and so on, depending on how you perceive their status in the industry. Using this metric, you can also look at your own CV (not your talent, presumably you believe your talent is A*), and think about what category you would put your CV in. If your CV is currently a B grade you may be more likely to get a response from pitching yourself to agencies on that level rather than to A* agencies.

When you're researching an agency, read about their ethos, mission statement and beliefs. Find out what you can about the individual agents who work there. An agent is a person, not a building; you're applying to them, not to a corporation. Find out about individual agents, read about their background, how they got to where they are, the type of people they work with and what they enjoy. Take some time to look at their social media. Ask yourself, would you want to hang out with them? Not only do you want to spend time with them, but would you feel comfortable chatting to them about personal problems, having a coffee with them or ringing them up for a natter? Do they seem like your type of person? Maybe think about companies in that way as well: if the company was a person, would you want to hang out with them?

Consider the length of time the agent has been in the business. The longer an agent has been working, the more established they are, therefore the more credibility and stature they have as an agent. An agency may be fairly new, but the agent running it could have had a long career in the business before setting up on their own.

Pay particular attention to how they like to be contacted. Some agents will specify they want to be contacted by email. Some prefer post, though that's rare in this day and age. Generally speaking, almost no agents want to be contacted via Twitter or other social media, so be professional in how you make contact and make sure you are adhering to their guidelines. Pay attention to how they ask for submissions and to what accompanying media they may be interested in receiving. Make a note of how they like to be addressed – when you're starting a relationship with someone it is always good form to get their name right.

During your research you might discover that the agent of your dreams represents a friend of yours, or someone you have worked with, or went to drama school with. You may be able to ask that mutual contact to recommend you. In an industry where who you know is as important as what you know, don't be afraid to ask for referrals. Ask your friends, directors, acting coaches and teachers. It may seem awkward or embarrassing, but a personal recommendation really can go a long way. It is always useful to ask for referrals or recommendations because so much of this industry is built on reputation. Your teachers, directors, peers and friends may have a particular idea of which agent could be right for you. Ask your friends what they like about their agents and what they don't.

Just as every actor is different, so every actor wants something different from their agent. It may be that communication is very high on somebody's list of priorities. Communication skills are often given as the number-one desirable quality in an agent, even above the agent's ability to get castings. For some, the *quality* of auditions may be the most important factor, for others it may be the *quantity*. It may be a posh office address or the agent's ability to purchase unique opening-night gifts. It might be their fair, competitive commission rates.

It could be any number of things, but use that information to build a picture of your 'perfect agent'. In the search for a perfect agent, though, just as in the search for a perfect romantic partner, be prepared to compromise. The chances of you finding someone with all the qualities you want straight out of the gate is unlikely. It's more likely that over time you will have different agents and each one will have a different quality and bring something different to your career.

Remember that choosing an agent is a very personal thing. Knowledge is power, so be prepared to research, research, research. Before you start to approach agents, work out what is important to you and work out what you want from them.

Contacting Agents

By now you will probably be impatient to start writing to agents. Hold back from this for a moment longer.

Your application is not simply about writing a good covering letter. It is a combination of a number of elements. Before you send an application you need to be certain that all those elements are working in harmony together. You are promoting a whole, unique package. Take a little bit longer to make sure all elements of the package are telling the same story.

If the agent you are applying to is not already familiar with your work in some form then, when encountering your application for the first time, there are three main elements on which they will base their decision to call you in or not: your headshot, your CV and your covering letter.

Some agents may look at your CV first, some will go straight to your accompanying media – your showreel or voicereel, for example. In an industry as visual as ours, most will look at your headshot first because how you look compared to other actors on an agent's book is a particular consideration.

At this stage we are not weighing up your material – an unsatisfactory headshot can easily be changed, a light CV is no reflection on your talent, a poorly edited showreel can be tweaked, etc. All the elements are editable and adaptable. We look at your headshot first simply because, when reading, our eyes work from the left-hand side of the page (or screen) to the right, so the way that Spotlight is formatted means a headshot is the first thing a casting director will see.

Your headshot

It used to be the norm to change headshots every six months. Once upon a time, Spotlight produced its legendary 'book' once a year. The book would sit on every casting director and agent's shelf for a year, so the headshot you chose would be the only visual reference they had for you for three hundred and sixty-five days.

Updating your headshot every six months meant that, halfway through the year, you had a reason to send a polite letter in the post to casting directors and agents reminding them of your existence. You had something to say. Nowadays, because Spotlight can be updated immediately online, you can change your main picture every month if you wish.

The trend for headshots is ever-shifting, but right now what casting directors want is fresh, natural and barely retouched shots. This is particularly important for TV, film and 'straight' theatre. You want great lighting and you don't want it to be too airbrushed. It should look detailed and three-dimensional, have depth and look real. For musical theatre, the trend seems to be to use a slightly more glossy picture in brighter colours with a bit more sheen and airbrushing.

Your headshot is your calling card, and from that picture we draw a lot of inferences about the type of actor you are. Too musical-theatre a shot and you will find it harder to get seen for TV or straight theatre. Too stylised a shot and, unless you're well known to the casting director, they may not take the risk on calling you in to discover whether you actually look like that.

> 'I just like a real, genuine photo that looks like you!'
> *Kharmel Cochrane, casting director, speaking to* The 98% *podcast*

Essentially, what we want is for the person who we choose to walk into the room to be the person we have seen in their headshot. If you can't roll out of bed and get to a casting within two hours and look like a pretty good match to your headshot… you've got the wrong headshot. If you have made radical changes in hair colour and style then do make your agent aware of this, as it may be a consideration. For the most part we appreciate that hair can easily be recoloured, braids and weaves can be taken out, or put back in, a buzz cut grows back, but if we are expecting a blonde pixie cut and a raven-haired emo arrives, you may have wasted your time. If it takes you six months to grow a beard then a bearded headshot is probably not very useful. Context is important – a low-budget commercial or fringe-theatre production happening in the next few weeks may not be able to use wigs, but large-scale productions certainly will.

In the past, the only way to be taken seriously as an actor was to be in the Spotlight book. We used to talk about the 'one killer headshot' simply because you only got one headshot published. In the days when headshots were shot on film you usually only got a contact sheet with thirty-two pictures on it. You may have been hard pushed to get any more than one decent shot out of them.

Those days are long gone. Now we look for a portfolio. Some people hold to the idea that this portfolio should present you as a variety of different characters. A range of shots would include a number of signifiers: brick wall = urban; hoodie = working class; tie = corporate type; glasses = quirky; and so on, and so on. This approach can seem a little dated. We want to see variations of you, not caricatures.

Have you ever seen those flickbooks that animators use? Different stick men in different positions on the corner of a page that, when flicked through, give the impression of movement? Perhaps think of the portfolio as suggesting that kind of motion, how you might look on screen from all angles, and select four slightly different angles with four slightly different intentions. Now that almost all photographers shoot digitally you'll probably find you have hundreds of great shots to choose from, many with only very subtle variations. Setting yourself the framework of four angles and four intentions can really help you narrow those down.

Choosing a photographer is a very personal thing. Do your research. Start with actors you know, see who did their headshots, and then expand that out to actors you admire. Think about that actor's career and whether they work in the field you want to work in. Notice the differences in style between musical theatre, stage and film actors. If there is a particular field you want to work in, choose a photographer who seems to work in that field. Does the photographer have a certain style? Will that style suit you? If you've done the work in the earlier section identifying 'Who Are You?', you'll know what you're selling. Perhaps a photographer that photographs lots of beautiful, sylph-like portraits might not be for you if you're positioning yourself as a more earthy, weighty person.

Some photographers might seem to work better with mature faces, others with younger. Some might appear more filmic, some more theatrical. Some photographers work beautifully with darker skin tones, some do not. Study as many sites as you can. When you have made your shortlist of favourite photographers, see what you can find out about them. Did people enjoy their session? Why?

Give careful thought to what you need to enjoy the session. Despite it being a necessary part of the job, many actors do not enjoy having their photograph taken, and sometimes that discomfort comes across in the shots. If you want a photographer who's going to have a cup of tea and a chat with you before the session, then make sure you seek out a photographer who works in that way. If you need a lot of direction, find one who works like that. Make sure that your session is as comfortable as you can make it.

Research is key and shouldn't be rushed. In marketing, every decision, every campaign, involves months of research, months of design, months of committee meetings. Your headshot is your company image – you should be absolutely certain that it is the best representation of yourself before you put it out into the world.

Be mindful of the image you are presenting. Learn to embrace your flaws and your quirks. Work out what angles suit you best. Practise those angles, practise posing in front of a mirror, practise with friends. Take pictures of each other, see which suit you best, and ask your friends to comment on what your pictures seem to say about you. Who are you? And what are you selling?

In many cases, the agent you are applying to has never met you before, nor has the casting director who has selected your headshot out of thousands. They are calling you in because, among other things, the packaging looks right. Make sure that the packaging matches the product when you walk in.

Later, when you have an agent and are looking for a new set of headshots, work with your agent prior to booking a headshot photographer. They will have opinions on what type of shots work best – ask them why. Ask what roles you are being put up for and what type of headshot will be most useful for them.

Lots of actors decide to make big changes to their appearance in the run-up to their headshots: losing a lot of weight, having a drastic haircut, growing a beard. Discuss all this with your agent before you do the same. Remember, your agent may not get to see you in person very often and they might have a specific opinion on your type and where they are pitching you in the industry. They can also advise you as to what difference this might make to how you are viewed and the type of roles you'll suit.

You should also consider whether keeping off weight after a drastic weight loss is possible. Will your body change shape once you leave drama school and are no longer running on adrenalin, dance classes and caffeine?

Give yourself time to get used to a haircut before your headshots. When you go from long-haired to short you may discover how much you love having shorter hair and want to go even shorter. If you have had new headshots done in the interim period, the result will be headshots that do not reflect your current look. Sometimes, after a radical change, you may not have had time to adjust to your new look or fully inhabit it, and the resulting headshots are timid and underwhelming. Bearded headshots are only useful if you're particularly hirsute and can grow one relatively quickly.

All this is, of course, how it currently works. Whether this is the absolute best way of working is debatable. Headshot photography, like everything in this industry, is a business. The need for a professional headshot is a requirement for membership of Spotlight, and for most casting sites, but is it a requirement for being an actor? Of course not. Search the internet for any guidelines on what makes a good headshot and you'll find hundreds, if not thousands, of articles on this subject – mostly written by photographers. Meanwhile, casting directors repeatedly assert that their primary requirement is that a headshot looks like you.

Much of this book was drafted on a phone, a phone equipped with a camera far superior to any camera that was used to shoot headshots in the past. Technology has advanced rapidly to the point where major film directors are shooting feature films on phones and huge pop stars are using them to make music videos. A recent cover of *Time Magazine* with Marcus Rashford was shot on an iPhone. The camera that many of you have in your pocket and take for granted is absolutely capable of shooting a more than decent headshot. What you are paying for with a headshot photographer is their time, their skill and their craftsmanship. The requirement of any casting site for you to have a professional headshot is a hangover from 'the way we have always done things' and does not reflect the modern industry. Increasingly, most headshots will only see the light of day in a theatre programme, and more and more we have noticed a trend for commercial theatre companies to shoot their own headshots in a house style.

We shouldn't do away with professional headshots altogether, but any industry that claims to be inclusive should not be encouraging graduates to spend hundreds of pounds on a picture to appear on a website. In recent years some headshots have become so stylised and reflective of the photographer's individual aesthetic that they have actually become off-putting to casting directors and agents. A headshot must be clear, detailed and look like you. How you achieve that and how much you spend on it is up to you.

You don't have to spend a fortune on getting the current hottest photographer to shoot you. You can achieve the same effect for a fraction of the price if you study the current in-demand photographer's style and compare it to cheaper, up-and-coming photographers. Or you can try to replicate their style yourself with good lighting, an online editing programme and your smartphone.

There is a tendency, among actors and agents, to examine the CVs of other actors to see who shot their headshot. It's a perfectly fine and useful exercise, with this caveat: extrapolating that this is the reason a certain actor gets booked is patently ridiculous. The best headshot in the world will not get you a job. Only your skill as an actor will do that. Your money would probably be better spent on continuing your acting lessons rather than on the most expensive headshot you can afford, which will inevitably be out of date in a few months' time.

Your CV

Let's look at an incredibly revealing document. The CV is one of the most useful tools in your package. Often it is the only thing a potential agent (or casting director) has, next to your headshot, on which to make the decision whether to call you in for a meeting (or an audition), or to pass you over. Knowing what an industry professional is looking for, and understanding how it is different to what your peers are looking for, is essential to crafting a great, eye-catching and noticeable CV.

What a CV *is* is a professional document to pitch you to an agent or casting director. What it *isn't* is a place to log every single performance, scratch night, one-off gig, monologue slam, cabaret, reading or R&D you've ever done. It is a marketing tool to promote you – either to an agent or to a casting director.

Remember that an agent sells and a casting director buys. It is your agent's job to polish your CV to make it attractive to the buyer. What is the buyer looking for? Diamonds. Don't make someone hunt through broken glass to find diamonds. Just show them the diamonds.

Your CV needs to tell a comprehensive story, but it also needs to tell the story efficiently.

For each credit on your CV, focus not just on the story you want to tell, but on who the audience is, and ask yourself: 'Why do I think it is important someone knows this about me?'

A good answer to that question would be that it mentions a great venue/director/company. A less interesting answer might be that it was a good part. The first is showcasing your diamonds to the reader, giving them something to connect to – a venue or director or company that they know. The latter is more about you than it is about the audience. Unless the part was at a venue they know, or in a production they heard about, directed by or starring someone they know, generally all a 'good part' reveals is that you can learn lines.

What is your CV saying? Is it a good example of the kind of work you're interested in? Does it demonstrate your taste? Is it revealing a lack of taste? Does it show the development of your career and interests? Is it reminding casting directors that your work is mainly short runs and short rehearsal periods, or is it emphasising the stamina you have built over long runs and lengthy tours?

Your CV is, if you like, an advertising billboard – it reveals more about you than you may realise. It is sent out dozens of times a day to people who spend eighteen hours a day, seven days a week, looking at CVs. It's their *job* to understand and interpret your CV. They usually know far more than actors give them credit for. They know which directors are great and will have stretched you, they know what the company you've been working for is like, they know roughly how much a venue pays, they may even know what the critical reception was. Even if they don't, the good ones do their research. An agent's job is to be well informed about the industry; don't underestimate that passion.

Even the best, most hard-working actor is probably only engaged in the business side of things for four or five hours a day, including performance time. Agents, producers, casting directors – they're involved all day, every day. They read social media and reviews, and trawl gossip sites and forums; they spend hours and hours understanding and talking about the industry. Put your faith in that experience. It's hard and it's scary, but trust in their professionalism.

Who are you? All the classes you take, all the one-off cabarets, all the short, unpaid runs of shows – these are part of who you are, part of your training and part of your development. But that doesn't mean they all need to go on your CV. That's like going to a car showroom and having the salesperson explain the inner workings of the engine to you when you just want to know what colour it is and what high-spec tech it has.

Just as on stage no one wants to see all of the work and preparation of rehearsals, they want the end product of performance, so with your CV no one needs to see the engine grease and oil – they just want the finished product, buffed to a shine and gleaming on the forecourt. The end product is *who you want to be* – or, at least, how you want to present yourself. A CV reveals who you are, but it can also give an idea of who you want to become. You may fancy doing a bit of stand-up, so you're taking a class and gigging around town. It's absolutely necessary for you to pursue all your interests, but if you want to be seen for classical roles at the Royal Shakespeare Company, then your CV will need to highlight credible theatre work and classical experience; a couple of nights at the local comedy club sharing an inability to orgasm as part of your tight five won't have quite the same cachet.

If you are not currently on Spotlight, it is a useful trick to lay out your professional CV so it looks like a Spotlight CV. Agents, casting directors, directors and producers have all very much accepted Spotlight as the industry standard, and so their eyes and brains have become trained to read CVs in a certain way. Copying the layout of the Spotlight CV will make sure all the information they are looking for is where they are used to seeing it.

After your personal details, height, location, playing age and so on, the first main section on Spotlight is the 'About Me' section. This is the first text we read and it is your only opportunity to write something personal about you. It is a useful place to draw attention to anything we are about to read in your credits, so highlight some work or an accent that may be on your showreel or voicereel, explain anything (like a large gap on your CV), or just tell us what you're currently working on. Think of it as an opportunity to refer the reader to something on your CV that may not be obvious, or to explain something that may not be clear: 'Amara's guest lead in *Casualty* this year can be seen on their showreel'; 'Micah recently played Frankie in *Up in the Sky* at the Edinburgh Fringe, gaining a five-star review from the *Guardian* for their "visceral, dangerous" performance.' It is a great place to actually tell us a bit about you: 'Rowan is a versatile singer with experience of cabaret. They are currently writing their second musical.'

An agent needs to be able to gather the maximum useful information from your CV in the minimum time. It is far better only to have your best work on there, even if it's just five credits, than to fill it with people, venues and shows people have never heard of. Just show the diamonds.

A diamond credit will usually fall into one of two categories, credits which are 'Recognised or Renowned' and credits which are 'Recent'. The most sparkling diamond will hopefully hit both. Some actors already have a number of diamond credits on their CV, but need to polish them a little to really make them shine. The largest rough diamond ever found was the Cullinan Diamond weighing in at over three thousand carats. Learn to polish the credits on your CV to make them shine as brightly as a three-thousand-carat diamond. Keep the focus on the 'Recognised or Renowned' and the 'Recent'.

A 'Recognised or Renowned' credit might be the most valuable one. An agent is building a picture of you professionally so they are looking for clues, things that tell them something about you. What helps is to highlight names an agent might recognise: venues, directors or companies. Sometimes all it takes is a tweak here and there to make the CV unlock its story. Lots of actors will list the production company rather than the venue. In many cases, though, the production company may be entirely unknown but the venue might be one we have heard of. Here's an example:

2019, Frankie, *Up in the Sky*, Turn Right Theatre Company

This doesn't say much. 'Frankie (Lead)' is a better character name than 'Frankie', as it immediately demonstrates not only the size of the role, but also suggests your experience at leading a company. You might also think about changing the name of the production company to the name of the venue. 'Turn Right Theatre Company' will be more revealing as 'Edinburgh Fringe' or 'Small-scale UK tour' – that tells us exactly what you've been up to. We know the Edinburgh Fringe, know what it means, know what it entails. We know the rigours of small-scale touring and how it works. Turn Right Theatre Company? Never heard of it.

You'd be surprised how much the venue name can reveal. We probably know the size, so have an idea of your technique, we may know people there, we might know something about the audition process, or how they like to work, or what they specialise in. We are learning something about you as an actor – which is what your CV is for.

Agents have generally worked with a lot of people. They know different styles and different working practices. They know who's on the way up, and who's going places. They know who is more traditional and who is pushing the envelope. They know different choreographers' styles and different musical directors' preferences. These names on your CV tell the reader a little about how you may have worked on a particular project.

Agents are pretty well informed, not just on the big stuff, but on the smaller stuff too. They like to keep an eye on new companies or young directors whose work interests them, whether they're working at the National Theatre in London or the Alma Tavern pub theatre in Bristol. An informed agent may very well have heard something about it on the grapevine. Agents are always chatting to other people in the industry and it may have been mentioned in conversation.

A fantastic example of this is the wonderful Hope Mill Theatre in Manchester. A relatively new venue, they achieved recognition and renown very quickly with a fantastic production of *Parade*. Casting directors, agents, critics and producers, who might otherwise not have made it to the end of the Victoria line, were suddenly hot-footing it Up North. In a very short space of time, the Hope Mill built on this to become a leading industry player. Perhaps your credit wasn't at a recognisable venue, or directed by a recognisable name, but if it was reviewed well and received well, then there is still a chance we've heard of it. As with everything, you can only work with what you've got.

Similarly, don't go so far with polishing your credits that it borders on an outright lie. For example, say you performed a Romeo monologue at the Globe during the Sam Wanamaker Festival, then be honest about that – don't try to suggest you played Romeo in a production of *Romeo and Juliet* at the Globe.

Agents interpret the clues you give them and that includes looking at when you last worked. They are looking at your recent work, but that doesn't necessarily need to have been in the last month, or even the last year. Your most recent credit should always be the top one on your CV, though, and hopefully that top credit will also be the most recognisable.

Don't worry if your most recent credit was a year or more ago. Agents are well aware there are many reasons people are out of work, especially in such a competitive market. The industry is filled with stories of those who landed a huge break just as they were about to give up because they'd been out of work for a few years. Everyone understands that this industry is tough and how unlikely it is for anyone, aside from the exceptionally lucky, to be in constant employment.

Think carefully about how many credits you have on your CV in any given year. A leading actor may have just one TV, film or stage credit a year. Having thirty stage credits and twelve screen credits in a single year will highlight that each project was very short and that your work on it was likely to have been small.

On the Spotlight website, if you are using tabs on your CV then the field you are most interested in should come first. If you are doing lots of work in TV and want to pursue that, then having stage or film credits first on your CV tells a different story. If you're a musical-theatre actor, having a list of all your commercials as the first thing we see isn't helpful either. Rightly or wrongly, it will be generally assumed that your first tab of credits represents your main area of interest and expertise.

Remember that an agent or casting director has the option to reorganise your Spotlight credits on the website. They may choose to read them in the order you have chosen – the tabs order – or they might reorder them by date so your most recent credit comes first. Make sure that, in whichever order they choose to read your credits, you are presenting the area you are most interested in as the top credits.

An agent will absolutely want to know about your skills, but if a casting director calls you in on the strength of your skill set, they're not looking for someone who can strum a chord or two or do a basic downward dog, they are looking for *skill*. Actor–musician productions are not looking for people with a Grade 2 clarinet certificate from thirty years ago, they are looking for actors to double as musicians. By all means let your agent know you can play a few chords on the piano, or not fall off a stationary horse, but please, please, please, only have skills you're actually *skilled* in on your CV.

If you are not competent and confident with a skill, take it off your CV until you've had the chance to work on it. No one will care if you can't do certain skills – it's far worse to claim you can do what you can't. Make sure too that your skills are relevant to the area of the industry you want to work in. You might have studied ballet at drama school a few years ago, but is it really a skill that's relevant to your future career in gritty, northern drama? Keep your skills up to date. As in any job, you need to demonstrate you are qualified, not show off as a mere enthusiastic try-hard.

Do remember that, although you might be a wild, creative flower, most of the people reading your CV are approaching it from a business rather than creative point of view. A lot of the guidelines for writing your CV are exactly the same as the guidelines for CVs in the 'real world'.

Check your spelling. This is particularly important on Spotlight. Casting directors can search Spotlight for certain things, like directors' names. It's not only disrespectful to a director when you get their name wrong on your CV, but a casting director searching for the correctly spelled version of a name won't find you in their search.

Keep your CV to two pages maximum. There is absolutely no need to have a CV spanning pages and pages. An agent does not need to know your entire employment history dating back to your childhood – even if you were a child star. Most roles you played ten or fifteen years ago are not representative of the type of actor you have become, nor should they be. Does 11-year-old you really look or sound anything like 20-year-old you? Have you not grown and changed considerably as a person and as a performer?

After a couple of years out in the world, take your training credits, if you have them, off your CV. You should have acquired better credits over time and those will hopefully be the credits that explain more about your interests and tastes as an artist than the productions you did whilst training.

A lot of actors write their CV 'for Mum and Dad', that is, packed full of credits that don't tell a cohesive story, don't reveal what they're really interested in and don't show how they see themselves – they are there because Mum and Dad loved them in that role. Actors often use their Spotlight CVs to show off work they are, rightly, proud of, but an industry professional is looking at your CV to solve a problem.

What if you are just starting out and you have no credits on your CV at all? Will an agent still be interested in you? It is undoubtedly harder to pique an agent's interest with a 'light' CV, and it is growing more difficult to attract attention without Spotlight membership. Casting directors are increasingly overworked, with myriad demands on their time. It is vital for a casting director to have all submissions for a particular role in one place – the Spotlight database – rather than having to sift through phone messages, postal submissions and emails. For this reason, many agents prefer only to work with actors who are Spotlight members, as it makes their process much easier.

But we all have to start somewhere. Whilst it is incredibly helpful to be a member and you may find it difficult to be taken on by agent without it, Spotlight membership is in no way a prerequisite for an acting career.

If you do not yet have Spotlight membership, there are still places you can find acting work. Other sites like Mandy, Backstage, Casting Networks, StarNow, CastWeb, Dramanic, The Stage, CastingNow, Flairbox and Shooting People also post listings of acting jobs on their websites. The quality of jobs offered on these sites is variable, however, and joining them all would be very costly. Perhaps try some free trials whilst researching which ones offer the most appropriate opportunities for your interests.

Some casting directors publish breakdowns on their social-media channels, and entering monologue competitions on social media, or the ever-popular Monologue Slam, is another way to get noticed, as these are often judged or attended by industry professionals. It is perfectly possible to build up a CV and body of work that will attract agent interest without already being a member of Spotlight.

Your media: showreels and voicereels

Your media package is increasingly important: showreel, voicereel, singing reel. Of these, in recent years, the showreel has become an essential part of your offering. The industry moves faster than ever before and a showreel where casting directors can see your work is a must-have for most people wanting to be seen for screen work. With so many thousands of actors to choose from for each role, so little time for auditioning and casting, and practically no time for on-set rehearsal, having a showreel that demonstrates your on-screen acting ability and camera technique is an important part of an actor's package.

That is not to say, however, that it must be professional, broadcast work. Nor does it need to be a professionally made showreel produced for you by a showreel company. When you are starting out in your career as an actor, you should not feel pressured into spending large amounts of money on having professional-looking material produced, nor should you feel disadvantaged by not having the means to do so.

A professionally made and produced showreel is a lovely thing to have, but its aim is to get you seen for professional broadcast work. As you book professional broadcast work you will be able to replace scenes on the bespoke showreel with your professional work. A bespoke showreel may, therefore, not last long if you are committed to pursuing a career on screen. Just as you knock credits off your CV as they become out of date, so too will you replace scenes on your showreel.

When you are just starting out, it is perfectly acceptable instead to use material filmed on your phone as a video clip on your online CV, or uploaded to a YouTube or Vimeo channel then sent on to an agent. In many ways this may be preferable, allowing you to choose your material carefully, knowing that it is specifically tailored to you. Something is better than nothing. If you have nothing else, then a short monologue can be useful. But since screen acting is also about reacting, it would be better to self-tape a scene with dialogue than using only a monologue. A home-made self-tape is just as useful and effective in the early stages. It should show how you look on screen, your acting ability and your camera technique. Everything else, lovely as it is, is just bells and whistles.

'When working on castings with a swift turnaround, I need to get a quick sense of what an actor brings to the screen. I'd rather they had a short, self-shot clip for me to view than nothing at all. I'm not interested in the production values of the video, I'm interested in the actor's performance. It may be that we're casting direct from showreel; so that self-shot footage could make all the difference!' *Wayne Linge, casting associate*

Some people might argue that, as self-taping has recently become a vital technique for all actors to have, demonstrating the ability to produce a good self-tape is actually a more valuable skill than spending hundreds of pounds for a bespoke company to produce a reel for you.

There is only one hard-and-fast rule for a contemporary showreel, and that is not to have a montage. We need to see you acting and reacting and we need to establish it fast. Take it from casting director Carolyn McLeod, who advises:

No one needs to know what you look like in an assortment of outfits set to a pulsing beat. A sense of dread comes over any casting director when they have to wade through a montage at the start of a tape.

If you really must have a montage then please put it at the end, so when an agent or casting director switches off your montage (and they will), at least they have seen the rest of the reel.

Good lighting and good sound are essential. You need to be seen and you need to be heard.

Whether you choose home-made or bespoke, a short showreel is best. An agent or casting director does not need to see an entire film, or be able to understand the full story. It is better to have several short clips that demonstrate your range than to have one or two longer scenes that show only one character.

> 'It should be no longer than your very best and most relevant material. Don't add average scenes to show you've done more work. Shorter is always better.' *Daniel Johnson, screenwriter and director*

Keep your clips short and allow your showreel to tell the story of who you are as an actor. You do not need to show huge variations of emotion, but it is unwise for every scene to be dramatic and emotional.

We are looking to see that you can act on screen, how you look on screen and that you have good on-camera technique. These are all things that you can practise on your own or with friends using a smartphone, and watching it back. Most people will happily watch a two-minute showreel, very few will spend four or five minutes watching.

> 'Be highly selective – only the best clips, don't hang on to old material or anything of variable quality. Make sure any scenes you include show the weight of the scene being about you, not your counterpart – we're looking to cast you, not the other person – and try to show a variety of clips where possible.' *Carolyn McCleod, casting director*

A good rule of thumb would be to make sure the first clip on your showreel is as close to who you are as a person as possible. You can use later clips to demonstrate your range and ability to act against type, but establishing who you are right at the beginning is very helpful. Establish yourself immediately by editing your first clip so that you are the first person we see and the first person to speak. Be interesting and entertaining, and do not be afraid to be different and quirky in your characters. Keep your audience in mind and remember to keep them engaged and entertained. It is very good practice to make sure that you are the first person to speak on your showreel; it establishes you in our minds straight away.

Old snobberies about commercial work have, for the most part, been put to rest, but if all your work is commercial it might give the impression that you are solely a commercial actor. The skill set for a commercial actor is often rather different to a TV and film actor. If the commercial is of a very filmic quality and tells a story, it can look fantastic in a showreel. If it is you turning cartwheels and eating yoghurt, consider creating a separate commercial reel. Using other reels is very useful if you are, perhaps, also a presenter or a motion-capture artist, or have combat skills. Keep the acting reel as just that – an acting reel. Make sure all your different reels are clearly labelled: 'Acting Reel', 'Commercial Reel', etc.

As you add professional broadcast work to your showreel, it can be a good idea to overlay the name of the project and the director on the clip. This not only enables us to match your work up with your CV and IMDb (your entry on the Internet Movie Database), but it also serves as a visual reminder of who you are working with and the calibre of the work you are taking on.

Many actors believe that a voicereel is an essential part of their package. If you are particularly keen on voice-over work – either commercial or audio-drama work – then yes, you may want to consider a voicereel, but it is by no means as essential as a showreel. If you have a particular gift for accents or speak a second language, a reel that demonstrates this will come in useful.

A good voicereel will demonstrate your ability to work, not only in commercial voice-over, but also in audio drama, audiobooks and, increasingly, gaming. Working in voice-over requires tremendous technical skill and vocal flexibility. Voice microphones are incredibly sensitive and learning the correct technique and refining your skill with a microphone is essential study if you are serious about voice work.

Voice-over work requires particular skills and techniques that are often not covered in detail at drama school, so it is highly advisable to pursue specialised training. As an area that is increasingly moving online and requiring home studios, it is not a field for a hobbyist; it requires investment, technical knowledge and a willingness to hustle for gigs.

Your social media

Love it or loathe it, if you use social media then it is out there for everyone to see and agents will look at it. Everyone knows that social media is important, although no one is really quite sure how important it is, or why. Rumours abound about the importance of your social-media following, and we have all seen breakdowns that specifically ask for 'large followings'. There are agencies who represent social-media influencers and there are, of course, a number of crossover areas. There are two main areas to address: how should you conduct yourself on social media, and is there any truth in the relevance of social media to the casting process?

Whilst it may seem old-fashioned, the most important element of casting is still assembling a cast who can actually play the roles and do justice to the work. In that respect, how many friends or followers you have is not going to be the thing that clinches it for you. Casting, however, is a complicated business. Many different factors will come into play and it is possible that one of these factors might be social media. The number of followers you have may be *one* of the considerations a panel looks at.

An essential question in casting is: 'What does this person bring that no one else can?' Your unique offering could be walking in the door of your audition serendipitously looking, sounding and acting exactly like the person the panel had in mind for the role. Perhaps, when it is phrased that way, you can see how very unlikely this is and how rarely it happens. Is it even possible that a panel of six or seven people could be imagining exactly the same person? Doubtful. Wouldn't it be wonderful if the 'best person for the job' was always cast? Sadly, the 'best person for the job' rarely exists. Casting is a committee decision; a producer, a director, a designer, a writer, sometimes even another actor who has already been cast, may all have an input into deciding who is 'the best person for the job'.

Casting has always included a number of variables. If you are auditioning for a musical, those variables will include your acting, your singing voice, your dance ability, etc. It may be, as in any audition situation, that you are better at one particular strand (dance, for example) than you are at others. When your suitability for the role is considered, your strength in dance might outweigh any weaknesses in acting. Similarly, your social-media following might be a factor for certain productions.

As many casting directors will attest, casting is more frequently a negotiation than a unanimous decision. A sacrifice may be made about how a character looks or sounds. There may, in a musical, be priority given to someone's singing voice over their dancing. It is a uniquely nuanced and complicated process, and one of the aspects that is under consideration could well be the height of your profile. Certain celebrities might be cast because a large following or existing fan base may bring guaranteed ticket sales.

Whilst a celebrity may receive special treatment, a kind word, or a more comfortable audition process, at the end of the day if the panel felt that they could not possibly play the role, they would not be cast.

Social media alone may not book you a role, but it can certainly lose you one. When we are beginning to build a social-media profile, our first fans and followers are, necessarily, our friends and family. This can lead us down the path of believing that social media is talking to people who support us, know us and understand us. As our social-media following grows we are increasingly talking to a wider audience, most of whom have never met us. This is when it becomes less 'social' and more 'media'.

A lot of successful social-media users will master the knack of speaking to followers as if they are friends. However, it is important to remember that when using social media you are broadcasting to the world. Social media is broadcast media. It is an opportunity to broadcast who you are and what you are interested in, so it's important always to maintain professionalism and dignity, and remember that it is permanent.

It is useful to ask 'What am I using social media for?' Are you using it to build your profile in the industry, to promote your work or to share your opinions? Depending on your reasons, you may find it useful to maintain two separate social-media profiles, one personal and one professional. If this is helpful then use your professional name for the professional profile and a nickname or nom de plume for the personal. Personal social media should only be shared with trusted friends and family. Professional social media should be used as if it were your own personal TV or radio station.

We are human beings first and artists second. We may say things in private we would not dream of saying in public. This is how we learn. We talk things over, we discuss things with friends and family, we listen to more informed and intelligent people, we take advice, and we use all this to form our own opinions. We are constantly growing and developing. Social media is a bit like puberty; we don't always want to be seen, it's spotty, smelly and uncomfortable. Just as we don't always want photographs of ourselves as teenagers coming back to haunt us, neither do we want old tweets or Facebook posts of opinions we may no longer hold, have outgrown, or thought better of, being used against us.

When using social media, consider adopting a consistent tone and style, one that represents you accurately. Who are you? How do you want to be seen? Social media can be used very effectively to underline your consistent offering, to support your brand. Essentially, you should expect your posts to be read, to be believed, and to be remembered.

The main social-media platforms (as I write this) are YouTube, TikTok, Vimeo, Twitter, Instagram and Facebook – and each of these can be used in different ways. All of them now have some kind of video-sharing element, from Fleets to Stories, but YouTube, TikTok and Vimeo are the main platforms where sharing content you create yourself can build your audience and get you noticed.

Instagram is mainly used for image sharing, and many actors use it to promote their artwork or visual projects, build an audience or express themselves visually. Instagram is perhaps the most aspirational of all the sites, heavily curated to showcase idealised lifestyle content. TikTok's primary use is for sharing short-form video content. Comedy and music work particularly well here, whilst YouTube and Vimeo both provide a space to upload longer form content, such as vlogs, tutorials or short films you create. Facebook and Twitter might best be described as personal news sites, the difference being Facebook can be limited to only the audience you select, whilst Twitter is broadcasting to the world. Twitter is frequently used for politics and opinions, but can also be used very effectively for short-form video content, perhaps driving an audience to a personal website or a video-sharing site to see longer content. Facebook can be used to build communities and advertise events.

Clubhouse is the latest social-media platform for creatives. Rather than a place to showcase your work, Clubhouse is a forum to chat, connect and collaborate with other creatives worldwide. Use Clubhouse to network and share knowledge.

The powerful thing about all these sites is the ability to interact with your followers and to form your own social community by responding to comments on your work. The downside of all these sites is the comments may not always be complimentary! As with any expression of creativity, social media requires a level of vulnerability; putting one's work out into the world is always terrifying. Learn how to filter criticism into what's relevant to you, what you can use to improve your work, and what to ignore.

Social media is a wonderful place to share and discuss your beliefs, to read, to learn, to show support and, crucially, to show us who you are. You can use social media as a professional way of getting your work in front of people. Using these platforms to demonstrate your creative skills as a developing artist can be incredibly beneficial to your career, so it is useful to have some overall guidelines that work across all social-media platforms.

In your social-media profiles or blogs, always include a link to your website or to your professional CV. If your social-media handle is not also your stage name, make sure your professional name is included somewhere in your bio. It is also extremely useful and respectful to include your pronouns. Be consistent and recognisable. Make finding out more about you as easy as possible.

Your covering letter

Here we are: you've worked out who you are, what your individual story is, and what it is you are pitching to an agent. Your headshot has been perfectly chosen to reinforce that story and captures your unique personality. Your CV explains and supports the journey you have taken thus far and is perfectly tweaked to highlight what's important, and expertly arranged to reveal its secrets. Finally, it is time to sit down and write that covering document which, for most agents (unless your research indicates otherwise), should be an email.

Agents can receive anything from ten to over two hundred emails a week enquiring about representation. In addition to all the other emails coming into an office, many of which require almost immediate attention, it can be overwhelming to have so many applications. Every agent will have a different way of dealing with them. Some may not respond at all, some may have a standard response set up, others may reply to each one individually.

Dealing with new applications takes agents away from their job – representing the artists already on their list. Knowing how to make your application stand out from all the others requires understanding what it is an agent is looking for and how best to present that to them.

From the first words, your cover letter should demonstrate that you have given care, thought and attention to the person you are addressing. Most agents have a biography on their website which will tell you something about them. Many have a Twitter account. Some post blogs or write articles about their work. An agent will be looking to find out as much as they can about you and you will expect your agent to be interested both in your work and in you as a person. As in any relationship, it is good practice for you to be as interested in the agent as you expect them to be in you.

The key to writing the cover letter is brevity – keep it short. Everyone in this industry is overworked and under pressure and looking for ways to reduce the daily workload. Keep to the point. Refer back to the work you completed in the first section of this chapter on knowing who you are and knowing what you're pitching to an agent. If you know precisely what your offering is, you can be direct and put it into the subject line of your email: '28-year-old mixed-race aerialist with strong stage credits seeks representation' is a great, attention-grabbing headline.

How do you actually write the email? You can say everything you need in three short paragraphs. The first paragraph need only be a line or two. It should say who you are and why you are getting in contact. If you have a personal connection, mention it during the first sentence – 'You represent my flatmate…' – or, if you know the recipient has seen you recently, 'You attended my showcase at...', etc. Do not say 'My friend Alex told me to get in touch', unless you are absolutely sure they know who Alex is.

Many casting directors have good relationships with the agents they work with, they know their taste in clients, and will often suggest a particular agent to an actor. If this is the case, and you are fortunate enough to have a recommendation from a casting director, then make sure you mention this in the first sentence. There is no need to begin 'I am writing to you today', as it is absolutely obvious that this is what you are doing, nor, if Twitter memes are anything to go by, should you begin 'I hope this email finds you well.'

The second paragraph is harder to get right. You need to demonstrate in about three sentences precisely why you think you are a good match for this particular agent and their particular book.

> 'I know you represent a lot of physical-theatre actors with strong singing voices, and are particularly interested in new writing. I trained in physical theatre, circus and rope, and have a strong baritone voice. I have worked with new-writing companies Theatre503 and Paines Plough.'

> 'I am a South Asian actor from Sheffield in the 30–40 casting bracket with good TV credits, and have noticed you do not have someone of my heritage in that casting bracket on your books.'

It is unfortunately true that most agents already have every casting type covered. Their priority is always to be sure that they are representing their current client list as diligently as they can rather than extending themselves too far. If an agent is looking for clients at all, then they are looking for clients they think they can help: those with a skill set they understand and have a track record in working with, those who have CVs that demonstrate they are working at the level they are looking for, or those who fill a gap that is unrepresented on their books.

The key points that your second paragraph needs to address are:

- Why are you relevant or right for this particular agent's book?

- Do you have an interesting skill set?

- Have you some recent news, such as a new role or new headshots, or have you just graduated?

Agents want to know three things: your suitability for their books, whether they have an opportunity to see your work, or whether you have some news or some recent professional change that might make you interesting to them. An agent does not need a précis of your CV as they can read that themselves, nor do they need to hear your life story. If you are called in to interview that is when you can share your journey so far.

The third and final paragraph should be no more than a line, thanking them for their time.

Most actors write very similar cover letters. Ninety-nine per cent of emails are almost identical. You should aim to be in the one per cent. The majority list similar things, tell a similar story and are indistinguishable from the rest.

Imagine you work in a large organisation and you're looking for a promotion. Right now you are at the same level as thousands of other people. Everyone at your level in this company has passed the same interview process – they have all demonstrated the exact same things: potential, passion, dedication. If you were asking your boss to promote you to the next level, would you do it by telling them you have exactly the same skills as everyone else? No, of course not. You would tell them what it is about you that is unique and what makes you different from the others. That is a good starting point to think about for your first approach.

Of the applications an agent receives each week, almost all will write about how passionate, hard-working, driven and full of potential they are. But these are the attributes expected as a basic requirement from absolutely every actor crazy enough to try to work in this industry. You will not survive without them.

As agents expect *everyone* to have those basic attributes, what they are looking for is actors with something that makes them stand out. Once you've worked out what it is about you that makes you unique, lead with that. Be specific. In a world where everyone with any musical-theatre training at all is claiming to be a triple-threat, why not be specific?

> 'I'm an outstanding dancer with a strong voice which makes me an excellent first or second cover in an ensemble. I'm not a Robert Houchen, but I'm well trained and I continue to work with a singing teacher weekly.'

Specificity. This tells the agent exactly what they will be working with, demonstrates an up-to-date knowledge of current musical-theatre voices, and tells us that you continue to train professionally – all in thirty-eight words.

An excellent exercise is the art of the concise redraft. Once you have finished your first draft, count the words then redraft, cutting the word count in half without losing any essential information. It is amazing how often you can do this, and it is an extremely useful exercise in discovering how much information you can pack into the fewest possible words. Your aim is to be precise and give as much relevant and pertinent information as possible.

Please get to the point as quickly as you can. Please redraft, reading it aloud as you go; this will help ensure that you are being as clear and direct as possible. A crucial part of acting is attention to detail and specificity. Use your covering letter as a way of demonstrating your attention to detail. Take a few extra minutes to read it aloud before sending, and run a spell-check over it. Bad spelling and grammar won't put anyone off, but it is relatively easy to go the extra mile and check and double-check before you click send. Your cover email is our first impression of you and how you present yourself, so try to make the best first impression you possibly can. If you find writing difficult then perhaps consider a short self-tape application that covers the information needed. You should feel confident in playing to your strengths rather than feeling excluded.

Include your headshot in the body of the email and not as an attachment. It does not need to be a large file either; the size it appears on your Spotlight CV should be absolutely fine. Let the agent see you straight away so they can tell if you are what they're looking for.

Always include your Spotlight webpage or link to your CV as a hyperlink: a link we can click on which takes us directly to the correct page. This is a tremendous time-saver and we will be grateful for it. If you are linking to your Spotlight page the correct format is: www.spotlight.com/XXXX-XXXX-XXXX-XXXX (where the Xs are the numbers of your View PIN) – anything else risks taking us to a log-in page which will take up valuable time. Please make it direct and as easy for us as possible.

Invite the agent to your show if you are in one and again provide a hyperlink, taking us to the company, or show website, if possible. There is no need to go into lengthy paragraphs about the production. It is great publicity for the show, but it is *you* the agent is interested in. If they are interested in you, they will look into the show. If they are not interested in you then no amount of describing what a wonderful experience, or what a fantastic part it is, will persuade them.

Remember *who* you are selling – make your pitch specific to *you*, not a production. Give the agent plenty of time. Agents have very full diaries and are unlikely to have space in the next month. The more notice you are able to give, the more chance you have of finding them with a free slot.

If you are not in anything, you should not necessarily be put off from applying to an agent, but do make sure you have something to say: 'I've just had new headshots done' is a good one; 'I've just updated my showreel' is another.

Many agents won't open or download attachments from people they don't know. If working from a laptop or home computer most people try to limit the possibility of inadvertently installing a virus. Therefore it is always best practice to send hyperlinks rather than attachments and, if sending a PDF version of your CV, to embed your CV into the actual message at the bottom of the email rather than as an attached file. If embedding a file is beyond your technical ability then include some of your best and most recent credits underneath your signature.

If you have properly researched the agent and agency, and are applying only to those agents you are specifically interested in, there should, of course, be no need to cut and paste. If you *are* using a cut-and-paste email then it is even more important to check, double-check and triple-check that you are sending the right email to the right person.

Really, getting an agent isn't that big of a deal and it is only a step on your journey, not the end of it. It should not affect your confidence or belief in yourself if you don't have one. There are many, many talented actors sat on agents' books, out of work. Getting an agent should never be the point at which you sit back and relax – this is *your* career and you must still be the driving force. Remember the analogy of working on the railways – your agent is laying the tracks but you are the driver. The direction in which you are heading is all your responsibility.

Reapplying, Staying in Contact and Networking

If the agent is not going to take your application further, it is not because they do not like you or don't think you are talented; it is most likely because they already have your type filled on their books, or they are not sure how to work with you to help you develop the kind of career you want.

How often should you get back in touch if it hasn't worked out the first time? There are a number of variables but, as a general rule of thumb, somewhere between six months and a year is probably a good time frame. Agents' books are rarely fixed – people often come and go. Staying in regular contact keeps you in the game. So many things in this industry are just good timing.

If you received no response, or just a brief one, perhaps wait at least a year. It is odd but true that time passes differently on this side of the table. Time seems to pass so slowly out there, waiting for the phone to ring, but on this side, six months ago can feel like last week.

One of the hardest things is learning to read between the lines. Quite simply, if the agent is interested in you, they will make the time to come see you or respond to you. If they are not interested, they won't. If an agent cannot make the performance they are being invited to, but they are interested, they will always ask to be kept informed of future opportunities to see you. If they want to meet you, they will manage to make time to meet you.

Getting in touch too often *will* bother people, though. Don't get in touch on Sunday, or over Easter, or on Christmas Day. Do you really want to be the actor that contacts someone on Christmas Day? A very good reason not to get in touch over weekends or holidays is because you don't want your email to be number seventy-four in a list that needs to be cleared from an inbox on Monday morning before work can actually start. An early to mid-morning email might hit just at the point where the backlog has been cleared and the agent is ready to move on and begin the day.

Remind people every so often that you exist, particularly if they've met you before. If you were nice and interesting, and a pleasure to chat to, most people will enjoy hearing what you're up to. December is an ideal opportunity to get in touch – even if you haven't seen or spoken to someone in a while; it's always nice around Christmas to remember people, which can open the doors to getting in touch more frequently when they might actually be able to work with you. It's also often quieter in the run-up to Christmas, so agents may have a bit more time.

Networking with agents is very scary for some people despite being relatively easy to do. You may run into an agent whilst you are out at the theatre, an industry event, or even a dedicated networking situation. It should be natural to meet and chat to people at these evenings. In fact, you can make it slightly easier on yourself by *not* thinking of it as networking, just think of it as meeting people.

Most people hate being 'networked', but if you see an agent at a party, or out at the theatre, then why waste the opportunity? As long as you are not attempting to trap them in a corner and spend twenty minutes trying to demonstrate how much you know about Shakespeare, or how much you know about the agent's personal life, or impress upon them how great you'd be for their client list, then you should absolutely feel comfortable enough to introduce yourself. Don't attempt to be coquettish and mysterious, don't be snide and arch, just treat the agent like a human being and behave like one yourself. There's nothing less interesting than someone trying to be interesting. Be interest*ed*, not interest*ing*.

Throughout your career you should be building your little book of contacts. This might include singing teachers, acting coaches, voice coaches, Alexander Technique teachers, accent coaches, directors, producers, casting directors, writers. Constantly be adding to that book. Twitter lists can be invaluable for keeping up with people. There are any number of Twitter lists you can find, and subscribe yourself to, to get updates from casting directors, producers or venues you admire and want to work with.

Agents should be on your list too. If an agent or any industry professional responds to an email, add them to your list. Frankly, those are the ones you want to work with anyway, they're interested enough in you to respond and polite enough to respect your time. If you keep up with agents, you'll be aware of when they are on the move from the company they were with. They may be looking to build a new list at a new company. Many agents have stopped agenting but gone on to become casting directors, writers or producers. Some have gone on to become Arbonne salespeople or estate agents. Who knows when they might one day be useful to you?

Lots of actors lose touch with their contacts after the project has finished. People move around fast in theatre, even faster in TV and film, and it's easy to lose track, particularly when you're busy. Regularly go through your contacts and update them. Who has moved to a different job since you last saw them? Keep your list current and up to date; how many opportunities might you be missing out on because you're not following someone else's career? This is a great thing to do once every two months – probably around the same time as you give your CV a quick refresh.

Interview

If you have been invited to an interview, congratulations! It sounds very formal, doesn't it? But an agent interview is really just a meeting and can take many different forms and many different formats.

Every agent is individual, every actor is individual, and every meeting is going to have its own individual flavour. Usually they are very, very relaxed, so you shouldn't have anything to worry about. They will most likely have already seen your work; at the very least they will have seen your material. Most important to remember, though, is that *they* have invited *you*. They want to meet you.

Where the meeting is held is as individual as the agency. Some agents roll out the full red carpet for new graduates, call them in to expensively decorated offices where they meet a hundred assistants, get made a latte by a specialist, enjoy a fresh croissant and a selection of biscuits. They are shown into a large meeting room with an oak table and headshots of famous actors on the wall. It is intended to awe them. Some schools even encourage their graduates to be impressed by this.

Other agents are more informal. Since the Coronavirus pandemic hit in 2020, more and more agents gave up their offices and worked from home. You may be taken for coffee or for a drink. Collective Agents, a large and very successful agency, was formed in a merger between John Rogerson from the Soundcheck Group, Boland & Reeve and Oxford Adams Associates – Oxford Adams' first office was in a boat on the Thames! Where the agency has its office isn't important; it's the content of the meeting that's relevant. Just because an agent has a fancy office doesn't mean that they're going to be better for you than an agent who is meeting you on a boat or in a café. As long as the relationship is strong and built on communication and respect, and as long as you feel that you're both on the same page and you're working towards the same thing, it really doesn't matter where your agent is working from. Every agent spent most of 2020 conducting meetings via Zoom. An agent can work wherever there's an internet connection.

You shouldn't worry too much about what to wear, nor should you feel compelled to put on any airs and graces. Don't dress as if you're at home, but certainly don't feel you need to impress or stand on ceremony. You are demonstrating who you are. It is your opportunity to be your best self, without being overly pretentious or made up.

Once upon a time, only a couple of generations ago, it was expected that an actor would wear a suit to an agent interview, but this is not a job interview, this is a meeting to begin a relationship. Be yourself! You are used to wearing different outfits depending on what the occasion calls for.

In drama school you're likely to have worn rehearsal blacks most of the time. You also have first-night outfits, clothes for your day job, clothes to meet friends in, clothes for formal occasions, family occasions, dressing up, dressing down. You're an adult and you're used to having different costumes depending on the scenario. For an agent interview, when you want to be relaxed and at your best, focus on being clean, presentable and, most of all, comfortable.

It's unlikely you'll be asked to prepare anything, although some agents do still ask you to bring prepared speeches and songs. The days when an actor was expected to have two contrasting monologues and two contrasting songs in their back pocket, primed and ready to go at a moment's notice are, mostly, over, and it's unlikely you'll be asked to audition for an agent during a meeting. Instead, you should expect the meeting to be a chat between two people trying to work out whether they have the same vision. It should never feel more weighted to one side than the other.

At no stage during the meeting should you feel you are being tested. You may be asked a number of questions but there is no 'correct' answer. Mostly, the agent is trying to get to know you, why you're doing this, what your ambitions are. We like to know what makes someone tick, what gets them excited, and what their journey has been so far.

Some agents might want to talk about your work, they may work through your CV discussing each credit with you. They may ask about directors you have worked with, names on your CV they recognise, or ask questions about particular jobs. They may ask where you see yourself in the future, what type of work you're interested in, and what type of work you're *not* interested in. It is not an examination and there is no pass mark you need to hit. They're simply trying to get to know you to see if you're a good fit for how they work and the type of work they see you doing.

Don't be afraid to have your own opinions. You don't have to agree with everything the prospective agent says, you don't have to have the same taste in theatre, TV and film. In fact, discussion, good rapport and the ability to banter ideas back and forth are quite important. It can be beneficial if your taste in art and practitioners is similarly aligned, but it's by no means essential. It's important you are honest about the type of work you want to do and the type of things that you see yourself doing, but don't feel you have to agree with the agent's opinion of the type of work you should be aiming at.

Try not to think of the agent as somebody you need to impress, but as somebody you're taking for a road test. Are you going to buy the car? Is this somebody you can get along with and will be happy talking to once a week for the next six or seven years? You shouldn't feel there is a hierarchical imbalance in the relationship, so you shouldn't be overly impressed by them or overly in awe of them. This is a two-way relationship.

Towards the end of the interview it's usual for the agent to ask if you have any questions. Having some prepared questions for this part of the interview is useful. Asking why the agent wanted to meet you can be a good thing, but be careful you're not phrasing it in a way that sounds as if you want to be told how wonderful you are.

Agents are essentially salespeople, so some actors like to solicit a sales pitch, asking 'Why should I choose you?' Be careful this doesn't come across as arrogant; remember that agents want to work *with* you, not *for* you. It's a really good idea to get to know the agent and ask them how they got into it and why they continue to be an agent. What's their favourite part of the job? What makes *them* tick? What makes them get up in the morning and want to do this day after day? Find out what it is that makes your agent want to be part of this industry. Again, be interest*ed* not interest*ing*.

Do ask about commission rates. This is a business relationship after all, so don't be nervous of discussing money. If commission rates seem strange or high to you, make a note of it and follow up with an email, or check with somebody else after the meeting. Many actors will want to ask whether the agent takes commission only on work that they have arranged or whether the actor is contracted to pay commission on all work, regardless of how it was obtained. There are many different viewpoints on this and, like everything, discussing it upfront is vital.

Ask how often you can get in contact with the agent. You may learn they don't want to have clients dropping in or calling them once a week. If you're just starting out and this is your first agent you may want an agent you can speak to regularly, or at least know that the possibility of speaking to them regularly is there.

You may want to ask what kind of career support or audition advice they give, and whether they see themselves as the type of agent interested in nurturing and developing your career. If there are specific fields you want to work in, such as motion capture, voice-over, animation, audiobook or commercial, you could ask about their experience in those areas. Ask whether they would be able to help you in that field or whether you need another agent for that. Ask if they are okay with you having another agent in those specific fields.

Ask if there's any work they don't want you to do, and be very clear about any work that you don't want to do. You may have reasons for needing to stay near to home, or not wanting to go abroad, or not wanting to be on a ship. You may be uncomfortable about nudity, or your politics may exclude wanting to work with certain companies. Be very clear what work you can and cannot do and what work you won't consider.

Some agents will like to finish the meeting with an offer and some may have a time frame for accepting that offer. Some agents may take a few days to think about things themselves. You should not feel pressured into giving an answer immediately after an interview. You should meet as many agents as have offered you interviews.

If you are in the fortunate position of being offered a lot of agent meetings, then you should go to a lot of agent meetings! Get a sense of the different styles of people. Even if your dream agent is the first agent you meet and they are the one you really want to sign with, you should still meet as many as you possibly can.

Before signing any contract, you should read it thoroughly – and, if you have a number of offers, you may find it useful to ask to look over all of the contracts before making a final decision. Agents' contracts can vary wildly, some are dozens of pages long, some are simply a page or two. If you are a member of Equity you can ask their advice. It can also be useful to have a look at the PMA website and their Code of Conduct. Some of the key things to look for in a contract are the rates of commission, the length of the agreement and how it renews, the procedure for terminating, and the scope of the agreement. For instance, do they represent you worldwide or just for the UK? Does the agreement cover all media or just theatre, or commercials? Is it an exclusive contract or can you have other agents?

If there is anything you do not understand, always ask the agent to explain before you sign. It may be possible to make adjustments or negotiate different terms before signing, but once signed a contract is a legally binding agreement.

When you are ready to make your decision, always make sure you let all the agents you met with know what your decision is, particularly if you're going somewhere else. Your paths may well cross again at some point in the future. An agent meeting is an opportunity to meet a useful contact in the industry and add a new networking name into your little black book. Who knows when that person may be useful to you, so always be respectful.

2. Keeping...

The Relationship

When you have secured representation with an agent, the next stage is building the perfect actor–agent relationship. This isn't about keeping your agent happy, but, like any successful relationship, keeping you both content.

Learning to develop a happy, productive relationship with your agent will reap rewards later in your career. Most agents will tell you that success takes time and that their most successful relationships are often the longest. Over time, an agent learns more and more about you and knowing you better is one of the secrets to good representation and submissions.

Hopefully this chapter will help to jump-start that relationship, moving it on to a point where you are working well with your agent, where you know what is expected from you and what you can expect in return. It is not only about you and how your behaviour can affect the relationship, it is also about what the agent expects, how you can help them, how you can help speed up getting to know each other's process, and what you should expect from them in the future. Signing with an agent is only one step, so this chapter will offer some guidance on how you and your agent can enjoy a productive and hopefully long-lasting relationship.

This stage is about developing as an artist, learning your craft, continuing your training, and demonstrating to your agent and to the industry that you have staying power and an ongoing dedication to your work. Committing to your career is a lifelong process and it is necessary to remain well informed about the industry, attend class regularly, network, meet and collaborate with other creatives. You should be stretching yourself continually, working outside your comfort zone, and learning and improving all the time. There's no race to get anywhere – but if there were, it would not be won by the fastest, but by whoever's still standing at the end. Like most industry relationships, building a relationship with your agent requires time and trust; it is built on trust, and trust is built over time. You build that trust together.

When you show up to an audition not looking like your headshot or not able to demonstrate the skills you claim you have, you have broken that trust. Being called to a casting, particularly in the early days of your career, is a mark of the trust that a casting director has in your agent, trust that has been developed over time, by your agent and their clients being consistent and reliable. On the flip side, an agent who sends you into an audition unprepared, with the wrong script, or at the wrong time, or for unsuitable projects, is breaking the trust you have placed in them to be your representative.

A casting director will often ask, 'Tell me honestly what they're like.' If the agent replies, 'They're brilliant, always on the ball, always prepared', and you show up late, messy, scatty, unprepared and unable to do what has been promised, then the relationship with the casting director has been jeopardised, and the casting director may wonder whether their trust in the agent has been misplaced. Every audition you go to is the direct result of someone else from your agent's list going in before you and impressing the casting director; actors from an agency are ambassadors for all the other actors on that agency's books.

Of course, things happen; people have lives, trains run late, families get in the way – we understand that, but all these things are nonetheless frustrating. However creative, however passionate the people you work with are, at the end of the day they are employing you to do a job, and they expect you to be ready and able to do that job – at all times. Being an actor is a lot of fun, but it is still a job. You need to know what is expected of you in this industry and be as ready as you can possibly be.

We build trust through communication, regular contact and sharing information that might be important to know. If you're developing an interest in new writing, or have decided to take your intermediate acrobatics up to advanced level, your agent needs to know. We need to know what excites you, what bores you, what interests you, what you want to learn, how your taste is changing, how your life is changing. Keeping track of your development is part of an agent's job.

The relationship between actor and agent isn't always business but nor is it quite a friendship. It is a transactional relationship, based on what each can do for the other. Agents invest a lot of time, money and effort into working for their clients – and often more so for those clients who are out of work. The understanding is that it will be repaid at some point. Few actors are in work constantly – you're not paying your agent commission for the job you are on, but rather you are paying commission so they will continue to work hard for you during the times you're not paying them anything.

Sometimes that transactional relationship doesn't quite click. All agents will agree that we often represent insanely talented clients who, for whatever reason, we find unable to get seen for the right stuff. Sometimes, with the best will in the world, it just doesn't work.

A lot of actors' jobs come from their own contacts. That's not to say your agent hasn't facilitated that. Hopefully they are keeping you out there auditioning so you always have something to say when asked, 'What have you been up to?' They are constantly thinking about how best to use each job to help you get your next one. An agent is working with you on your entire career, not just on the jobs they have direct involvement with.

Being proactive in your career is not only recommended, it is essential. Your agent's career is managing a number of actors; to be an effective agent they must have some responsibility towards their own career. Your career is your responsibility. Even with the best agent in the world, you cannot sit back and expect them to do all the work for you.

Remember that other creatives – directors, producers, etc. – work directly with actors. They understand them and want to work with actors who are proactive and forward-thinking. You're not in the rehearsal room with your agent, you're not out on the road with your agent, you're not spending your days with your agent – you are spending your time with other creatives. This is your network, your tribe, these are the people you want to think highly of you, to recommend you, to trust you with work. If you're sitting back and expecting your agent to find all your work then you've fundamentally misunderstood what your role in your own career is.

Before email and mobile phones, it was incumbent upon the actor to get in touch with their agent on a daily basis, usually late afternoon, hoping against hope that an audition might have come in for the next day. Now, of course, with all the communication available to us, there's no need to call up every day. Whilst this does have its upside for busy agents, the downside is that actors now don't have cause to call up, and the whole tradition of checking in with your agent daily has gone.

There are still many credible reasons to get in touch with your agent on a regular basis, not least because it reminds them you exist. It's uncanny how often a client emails at precisely the right moment, just as a brief that's absolutely spot on for them arrives in the inbox. Keeping in regular contact with your agent keeps you always on their mind, but it's good to agree the parameters early on. Discussing your needs and wants early on in the relationship is a good idea for both parties.

Remember, you're not the only client your agent has, so the onus of putting in work on the relationship falls mainly to you. Your agent is a human being too, with on and off days, a need for a holiday, a personal life. Agenting is just one part of their life. They may have other interests, hobbies and passions. Allow them to have those, and try to respect their time.

Your agent is not is a lawyer, and they are not a financial adviser. It is in your interest to have separate financial advice from an accountant. However experienced they are, your agent is not qualified to give you legal advice.

A key part of the relationship is that your agent takes care of the finances of your work from, hopefully, negotiating your fee through to invoicing and collecting it. Your salary is received by your agent, their commission is deducted, you are paid the remainder, and they provide you with a remittance explaining what deductions have been made.

VAT (value-added tax) is a tax on goods or services. If your agency is over a certain size, and is registered for VAT, then it is a legal requirement they charge VAT. This is charged on the service they provide, which means you pay VAT on the commission.

Equity can give you advice on contracts, if need be and if you are a member. For the peace of mind that Equity membership affords you, the legal assistance and financial advice they offer, it is a fairly essential service and, if you can afford it, worth the membership subscription. It is in your interests to have Equity as part of the team of people you can turn to for advice.

Auditioning

An audition is your opportunity to be an ambassador, not just for yourself, but for your agent, for your agency, for your CV and for your reputation.

An audition is not an opportunity to get a job, rather it is an opportunity to show how you would play a certain role if given the chance. The difference is between trying to *get* and trying to *give* – knowing who you are and what makes you individual is the key to knowing what it is you have to give and what you have to offer.

An audition is an opportunity to show what you can do. An opportunity to show where you are at this particular stage in your career, to give a snapshot of where you are at this particular moment in time.

Many actors judge their agent by the number of auditions that they get. Whilst this is, of course, an important factor, it is also important to think about the quality of auditions. It may be that you are being seen for a large number of commercial auditions, but that's not where you want to be. Quantity of auditions is not the sole barometer of a good relationship.

Think also about the quality of the meeting and not just the quality of the opportunity. The meeting itself is important. Are you meeting the right people for your career? Sometimes you're meeting a casting director and you may not be right for this specific project, but you may be right for them for a later project.

Your goal at an audition is to make enough of an impression to get another audition. That other audition might be a recall for the same project or it might be that you impress enough to be called in for another meeting for a different project. Going in for a lot of unsuitable jobs is not the same as going in for a handful of castings that are specifically right for you, castings that you really want, that you burn for, that you think, 'I really want this, I live and die for this', as opposed to playing Brown-Haired Girl No. 25.

In a perfect world, an actor's job is to act. For most actors, a large part of their job is to audition. Auditioning improves technique and discipline and keeps you in front of casting directors. For most actors, auditioning is a necessary evil. It is probably best to make your peace with it as early as you can. You will likely audition more than you work, certainly in the early days.

Many actors might be in two minds about a job, but decide to go to the audition, find they really hit it off with the team and completely fall in love with the project. Conversely, many actors are desperate to work with someone, only to meet them and realise it's not for them after all. If you're in two minds, go to the audition, you never know where it might lead. The time to turn down a job is when it has been offered, not before. If you go to the audition you might not be offered the job, but if you don't go, you definitely won't be. That said, if you absolutely can't, or wouldn't take the job, then don't take an audition slot from someone who could.

When you receive an audition notice from your agent, they will expect you to get to work on preparing whatever you have been asked for: songs, monologues, scripts, scene work. They also trust you to do your research on the team you will be meeting. This includes researching the casting director, the director, the production company, reading the play, and so on. This will not only help in the audition (that awful 'Any questions?' moment; if you have done your research you should have a couple of questions ready to go), but, more importantly, will help you come to a decision about whether this is a company and creative team you want to work with.

Keep your skills up. Keep everything fine-tuned and ready to go at a moment's notice. It's easier to *stay* ready than it is to *get* ready.

Only a few years ago it was expected that you would have a 'monologue' folder of appropriate pieces. Although this practice has largely fallen out of fashion, monologue work is still useful, as it is something that can be done at home on your own, as a way of working on your craft. You'd be covered for most emergencies by having one monologue in your repertoire in each of the following styles:

- Modern British
- Modern American
- Classical
- Comedy

A musical-theatre 'rep folder' is your repertoire of songs in a variety of genres prepared and ready to be performed for an audition where you're required to sing. It's a little more complex, but a good, basic list would include:

- Sondheim
- Contemporary British musical theatre (2000–present)
- Contemporary American musical theatre (2000–present)
- 'Legit' musical theatre (US or British pre-1960)
- Pop/rock

And preferable, but not essential:

- Jazz
- Disney
- Classical
- Folk
- A capella

Recently, other terms have come into vogue, such as 'contemporary legit'. Whilst 'legit' is usually a reference to the period known as the 'Golden Age' of musical theatre (the period pre-1960), many composers have continued to write in the legit style, giving rise to the term contemporary legit. It may therefore also be useful to include a contemporary legit piece in your folder.

It used to be a requirement to have two contrasting songs in each of these categories, and actors would often be asked to 'bring their rep folder'. Never have anything in your rep folder that you could not sing at the drop of a hat. You can be sure that if a musical director were to leaf through your folder, they would pick the one song that you're not so confident with, so if you can't do it, don't have it in there! As producer and casting director Danielle Tarento says, 'Your only job in a first-round audition is to get a recall.' Make sure your choice is demonstrating your skill to the best of your ability so as to guarantee the panel want to see more of you.

Post-Covid, it has become increasingly common for actors to be asked to email PDF versions of their chosen audition songs over to the panel before the casting. It is a very useful, time-saving practice to have your sheet music scanned in, saved and ready to go. Do keep it updated; you'd be amazed (or possibly not) how many people are still singing *Into the Woods* when asked for a *contemporary* musical-theatre song – it was written in 1986.

Sometimes actors take the same material to an audition for years because they know that they perform it well. What can happen is that it becomes habitual, and your choices become repetitive instead of imaginative. Something that worked well for you in your twenties may not land quite so authentically in your thirties.

Thorough preparation is going to help you with confidence; it will mean you have one less thing to worry about. When you're in the room all you can control is your own behaviour. You can't control how the panel feel or whether the audition is running late. You can only be in command of yourself and in the decisions you are making. Control the controllables.

Your Audition

When does the audition begin? Lots of people will say that it begins from the moment you enter the audition building – but an audition begins when you leave the house. You never know who is going to be travelling with you, who is going to see you on the way there. You certainly don't want to get into an argument or burst into tears in front of someone on the bus, only to find them seated behind the table when you get into the audition room. Start mentally preparing for an audition the moment you leave the house, thinking yourself into the right frame of mind.

Knowing your own process for dealing with audition-room nerves is important and is something you develop the more you audition. Some people like to be completely focused in the waiting room, quiet and still. Others love running in to friends and find that chatting with them can help allay their nerves.

Know your own process and preferences, but be mindful of others' too. You may find it helpful to do a full vocal and physical warm-up in the waiting room, but there are likely to be other auditionees there who find this off-putting.

Agents will often have picked up tips over the years for coping with audition-room nerves from the many clients they have seen go through similar situations. Don't be afraid to ask for advice. Remember, too, that an agent will likely have seen many clients go through all kinds of different auditions. If this is your first West End audition ask your agent what it will be like. If it's your first time in front of the Royal Shakespeare Company, ask what to expect. Agents have a wealth of knowledge and experience when it comes to auditioning: use it.

You are a human being first, and an artist second. Sometimes things are happening in your life that may have an impact on the energy you project in the audition room. This can have an impact on whether a casting director wants to call you in again. Everything happening in your life can have an impact on the energy and the appearance and the attitude that you give off in the audition room. If you feel you are not at your best then assess whether external factors are contributing. Remember, there are so many things about the audition process that are out of your control. Focus on what is within your control.

'Go into the audition room and be open and friendly, listen to what is being asked of you, make the adjustments you're being asked to make, be professional, and then when you leave the room – let go of the outcome.' *Jim Arnold, casting director*

Like any performance, an audition is an opportunity to communicate. Acting is storytelling, communicating that story to the audience. Too often we forget this, and acting becomes about our own individual performance. So intent are we on being noticed by the producer we know is in the stalls that night, or attracting the attention of the new agent we're desperate to sign us, or getting spotted by the casting director we've heard is watching the show, that we forget our role, our job, which is to communicate the story.

'What's key is never to "see" the acting. Don't look to impress or show how hard you've worked. Don't be memorable – be authentic.' *Sophie Holland, casting director*

This can be so hard to do in an audition situation! We're trying so hard to show off all our talent, all our preparation, all our enthusiasm for the part, we forget to communicate the story. If you can't communicate the story in a room with just you and a handful of other people, how are you going to communicate the story to an audience?

Above all, please remember that you are now working in 'the business'. Yes, it's creative; yes, it's fun; but at the end of the day, it is a business and you are an employee. Be as professional as you would be if you were working in a bank or a law firm. If you present yourself professionally you'll keep your agent happy. It's not about always booking jobs. There are multitudes of reasons why someone doesn't book every job they go for. It's about consistent professionalism – and a bit of fairy dust.

'You did your best that was on offer for today. You may not have been right for that role in that show; however, one day you will be right for something else that office is casting, or the director could be working on another project and think of you! And if they don't, that too is fine. You need to not be down on yourself every time you don't hear back from an audition or self-tape.' *Sonia Allam, casting director*

In most cases you will not be expected to be 'off-book' at a first audition, and holding the script is a useful visual reminder to the panel that you have not had long with the material. Of course, context is everything. If it's two lines then you should probably learn them, but an audition is not a memory test. Better to spend your time feeling your way around the scene and fleshing out your character than memorising by rote. If in doubt, ask your agent to check for you.

After Your Audition

Keep a notebook of all the auditions you go to, recording what they were for and how you felt about them. This way you start to build a picture of what you are enjoying and what you're not enjoying. This will also help you to discuss your progress with your agent. Keeping a log of what you wore, what material you brought and who you met is a great habit to acquire. Having a brief record of these things is useful so you can check back and remind yourself of what worked and what didn't, what the casting director was like, who was in the room... A log doesn't need to be complicated, it can be as simple as:

- Project
- Date/time
- Venue
- Who I met
- What I wore
- What I was asked to prepare
- How I thought it went
- Any other notes

It used to be standard practice to check in with your agent after each audition. It's another way of being able to keep in touch, to have a reason to contact them, rather than just calling up on spec. It's also really helpful for them to hear what you enjoyed about the audition and what you didn't. They are usually sat in the office staring at a computer screen whilst you are out there meeting people, going to castings, going to auditions. Feeding back is a very helpful habit and another means of keeping in contact.

It is good to discuss with your agent any notes you may have been given whilst the audition is fresh in your mind. There's such a rush of adrenalin that comes with auditioning that often you come out and don't really remember what just happened. Have you ever had that experience of performing where you've been totally in the moment and afterwards everything seemed a bit of blur? Whilst you may find that a highly desirable state to be, it can also mean that important information is forgotten.

This is when having your audition notebook comes into its own. As soon as you come out of an audition, jot down anything that was said to you. This is a particularly useful practice for any audition where you might be getting a callback. You might have been given some suggestions in the room for things you need to work on. Note it all down whilst it's still fresh in your mind. If you call your agent, you can also share this information with them. If your agent discourages this practice, then pop it into an email and use that as a way of focusing and concentrating on what's just happened in the audition.

Reflecting and making notes can be difficult and uncomfortable if the audition has not gone well for some reason, but it's even more important then. Creatives have a tendency to brood on what they perceive as negative information. This tendency is called negativity bias. You may have been given five compliments in the room, but you'll overlook all the compliments and focus on the one statement you perceive as negative. Talking it through with your agent as quickly as you can helps to end the practice of negativity bias.

An audition is part of the process of being an actor and you should try, wherever possible, to make it part of your learning process. A bad audition does not mean you are a bad actor. It may mean that you may have made a bad choice in some way or it may be that you are overthinking. Talk through the choices that you made and how you felt, and see if you can analyse why the audition felt bad.

If you imagine an audition as a pie chart, you can start to see how the audition is made up of many kinds of different elements. Getting all the words right may make up one large chunk. Hitting all the right notes. Being on time. What you wear. Remembering your own name! Imagine all the elements as percentages of the whole noting that these will be different for every audition. All of it adds up to one hundred per cent. Don't focus on the one per cent you may have got 'wrong'.

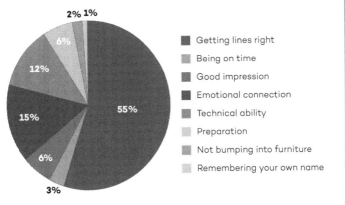

2% 1%
6%
12%
15%
55%
6%
3%

- Getting lines right
- Being on time
- Good impression
- Emotional connection
- Technical ability
- Preparation
- Not bumping into furniture
- Remembering your own name

You should also never be worried that your agent is going to be upset or angry with you after an audition (unless you behaved badly, of course). If they *are* upset or angry that you don't get a recall or book the job, then perhaps you're with the wrong agent. You should always be learning, you should always be thinking about how you can develop from an audition, always be assessing what did or didn't work for you. Your agent can be part of that process of reflecting, evaluating and learning.

Talking it through helps you to understand how your choices can affect your behaviour. Maybe you tried something new in this audition – a new approach, a new technique, a new way of preparing or some new material – and maybe it didn't quite land because it takes time to build your confidence in new practices. Often the first time we try something it doesn't work because we are nervous and insecure with it. It can take a while for things to bed in and feel comfortable. Talking through why it didn't work can help you discover solutions for next time.

It is a rare agent that has the time to work through audition pieces with their client, although it is certainly not unheard of. As self-taping has become more commonplace, though, it would be very unusual for an agent not to watch your tape before sending it off. It can be incredibly useful, particularly at the beginning of your career, to have some feedback from your agent. After all, an agent will usually be watching a number of tapes every day and will have developed an eye for which ones are getting the client called in or booked on a job. Some agents will routinely request your tape a day or two before the deadline so they can watch it and suggest adjustments if necessary. It is not always possible, given the very fast turnaround for many tapes, but remember your agent *wants* you to book the job, so do ask for advice and guidance where you need it.

Increasingly, auditions are via self-tape or online, and sometimes, when you're working from your bedroom, it can be easy to forget that the same rules of auditioning apply. There are also all kinds of new considerations with auditioning online. Think about what's visible behind you, on the walls, on your bookshelves, make sure your internet connection is strong, try (if you can) to ensure you won't be interrupted and wear something appropriate. It may be a character choice to audition in your dressing gown, but it's unlikely to come across that way. Make sure any comedy filters are switched off, and that your correct name is visible.

When emailing or uploading your tapes, always, always, always make sure you change the file name to your name so that it doesn't get lost in amongst thousands of submissions.

Nurturing the Relationship

A common concern is how often you should get in touch with your agent. If you are not out auditioning frequently, you will not have the excuse of asking for advice in preparation or of checking in afterwards. If that is the case, then a good rule of thumb is to get in touch when you have something to say.

A busy and productive actor will find they often have something to say: if you've done a workshop, if you need advice on who to go to for new headshots, what to include in a showreel or voicereel… These are perfect reasons to send that email or make that phone call to your agent.

It's sometimes useful to get in touch if you've heard about something on the grapevine – perhaps you've heard that a show is casting or a production is coming to the UK.

Agents love receiving information; it's how we build our knowledge and our skills. We are, of course, constantly learning, reading blogs, social media, newspapers, magazines and trade journals. We are always talking to people trying to find out what is happening, what's coming up, what trends there are – it's all part of our job. That said, it's maybe not a great idea to phone up just to ask why your flatmate is in for something and you aren't – unless your flatmate happens to be your identical twin, there's probably a very good reason.

How often you should keep in touch is something that should be discussed in the initial interview. However frequently or infrequently that is, an actor should never be scared, nervous or worried about speaking to their agent. Working with your agent means developing a professional relationship, working together towards the same purpose. The relationship is not always equal, though; whilst you may know yourself very well, your agent may be more experienced in the business side of the industry than you. Just because the relationship may be unequal, it does not mean it should be without respect.

In quiet periods there is a temptation to contact your agent frequently and ask what is coming up and what auditions you are likely to be called in for. Sadly, few agents are fortune-tellers. An email asking why it's so quiet for you can feel like a personal attack. Agents are always working as hard for you as they possibly can. Often this work is almost invisible to the actor. You're not in the office whilst your agent makes phone calls on your behalf, sends out your CV, submits you for jobs, talks you up, thinks about you and pushes you… So much work that doesn't result in an audition (yet). At the beginning of your career, your agent is making many introductions on your behalf and that work will pay off in time, but it can often take quite a few pushes on the part of your agent before a casting director agrees to audition someone. Your agent's business depends on you working. It is in their interest to keep you in work. It is in their interest to keep you happy. It is in their interest to keep you feeling creatively fulfilled.

It is generally more useful, and will net you a more detailed answer, if you ask whether there is anything you can be doing during the quiet period. Asking how you can work better with your agent is always going to be received more positively than inferring they are not working hard for you. Perhaps ask your agent to share any insight they have about how the industry is progressing.

Working with your agent in a positive way allows your agent to see you an asset. An agent's clients are passionate, intelligent, committed and creative people. Most agents learn as much from their clients as their clients learn from them.

> 'Being proactive is more important than ever in the times we are living in. I always support actors when I can, who feel like they may need to send an email, or keep their skills sharp with a Q&A, or reach out for advice and help in order to try and get their foot in the door. Working alongside your agent as partners, and both being proactive together in sync and in a coordinated way, is equally if not more important.' *Heather Basten, casting director*

Every year at Christmas, it seems to be the trend for agents to spend a lot of time on Instagram and Twitter posting pictures of the wonderful presents they have received from their clients. Whilst all agents do, of course, appreciate being sent doughnuts, chocolates, flowers, plants, gift vouchers, five-star Mediterranean holidays... none of this is necessary. Your agent knows precisely how much money you have earned in a year from your creative work. By all means send a gift if you want to, but it should in no way be considered to be an essential part of the relationship.

Over time, your relationship with your agent will change. Your agent gets to know you better and this can often lead to an improvement in the type of work you do and the type of roles you go up for. You may come to think of your agent as a friend. It is certainly not unusual for agents to become godparents to their clients' children, to attend their weddings, to become a trusted confidant. However close you grow to your agent, do not forget that the relationship is a business one. If the business side of the relationship is not working for you, you may have to think up an exit strategy that ensures you retain them as a personal friend, even if you no longer work with them on a professional level.

Moving on from an agent can be a traumatic and upsetting experience on both parts, though. A later section of this chapter offers some best-practice ideas for minimising the difficulties.

Updating Your CV

Keeping your CV updated is a vital part of your job. This is something you should work on with your agent, but essentially it is your document for selling yourself. It is your front page, your advertising brochure. Keep it up to date, keep it relevant.

During 2020, when the creative industries were at a standstill, very few people had anything recent or relevant to add to their CV. However, as lockdown restrictions eased, it was apparent that the people who used the 'About Me' section to talk about what they had been up to during that time seemed to be the first people called in for castings. Your skills can become rusty very quickly if they are not being used, so it is a very good idea to use the 'About Me' section as a way of demonstrating that you continue to hone your abilities.

As the number of people working in the industry increases (and the work does not), your 'About Me' introduction becomes a useful marketing tool to promote yourself. Use it to talk about skills you are acquiring, projects you're working on away from acting, even letting readers know of any new life experiences, like a marriage, a child or a temporary career break. Think of the section like the logline for a movie – a snappy sentence or two which sums you up. It's your space to give the reader a little personal insight into your world.

As you develop and your CV gets stronger, as your credits become better, discuss with your agent what work is relevant to keep on your CV. Student and graduation shows very quickly become irrelevant. Your student shows should be the first things to come off. As you add one credit to the top of the pile, knock one credit off, so your CV is constantly fresh and up to date.

Be judicious in which credits you take off. Don't, for example, take off a stint at the Royal Shakespeare Company or the National Theatre in favour of a fringe show you did simply to remind yourself you're still an actor. Remember, the aim is, over time, to build a CV of diamond credits that demonstrate your interests and versatility. This does not happen overnight; it is a long process. Always have what you're currently working on as the top credit, but keep the rest of the credits focused on showing off your diamonds. Don't knock something off simply because it's old – only knock it off if it becomes irrelevant.

At some point in your career you may want to change focus. You may feel you've done too much musical theatre and you want to move into straight theatre. Maybe you want to explore moving into TV and film. Perhaps your CV is overloaded with commercials and this is all you get called in for. Learning to focus your CV is a very, very useful skill. If there are a number of theatre credits and you want to sharpen the focus on the short films you've done to present yourself as a screen actor, then judiciously cut down the smaller theatre credits and leave only the best ones. No one is going to be upset that you're not using your professional CV as a comprehensive catalogue of your entire career, and your agent should certainly be keeping a complete record of all your work, training and meetings.

If you don't want to be seen as a commercial actor, don't put every single commercial that you've ever done on your CV. You can just include a couple to remind casting directors and commercial casting directors in particular that you are capable of booking commercials. Once you're out of the 'conflicting' commercial period, you might want to take a commercial off so you can book a new one. For example, say you were featured in a supermarket commercial and so weren't able to appear in a commercial for a competitor for three years, once the three years are up you may want to free yourself up again for another supermarket. Taking credits off and reordering your CV helps to make the diamond credits shine. Two theatre credits and one short film buried in among thirty commercials make it difficult to pick out the theatre and screen credits. Work with your agent to decide which credits are not serving you and when is the right time to take something off.

'Versatility' is a word that is often thrown around; almost all actors want to be seen as versatile. However, versatility s something to work towards and aspire to. It is not automatically assumed. A great screen actor does not necessarily make a wonderful stage actor. A brilliant commercial actor is not necessarily a gifted TV actor. The industry will not automatically assume that a strong comic actor can also be a strong dramatic actor. These are all skills that need to be acquired. Your CV is a flexible, ever-changing document that reflects where you are on your journey. It needs constant attention to ensure it is always an accurate representation of where you currently are on your path, and to indicate the direction in which you are travelling.

Set a calendar reminder every two months to give your CV a quick refresh, so that it stays up to date all year round. Double-check that no spelling mistakes have slipped through, and tweak and refresh the listings to make sure they're staying relevant.

It is also useful to check your CV during quiet periods, to remind yourself of the good work you have done. If you've worked before, you will work again. Sometimes it can seem as if everything has dried up and withered away. Try using your CV to lift your spirits and to help you visualise the type of work you want to do. A useful exercise is to imagine you are a director or a casting director and to read the CV as if it is the first time you have ever seen it. Remember – an agent sells you as a product and a casting director buys. Is it clear what's on offer?

It is scientifically proven that writing something down is one of the best ways to visualise it happening. Writing and focusing on TV and film credits can really help you visualise yourself booking more TV and film work. Writing down your theatre work and focusing on the good theatre work you've done in the past can help you visualise booking more theatre work in the future. Work begets work, and in most cases the same work begets more of the same. Use updating your CV as a powerful visualisation technique. Look at how far you have come and what you have achieved – and visualise where you want to go next.

Moving On

It is sad but true that at some point the time will come to leave your agent. Perhaps this has come about by your own volition, or perhaps it has come from your agent. Changing agents is something most actors do a number of times, and it is increasingly rare that one agent will be by your side for the entirety of your career. So, whilst it may seem incongruous to discuss how to leave an agent in a book titled *Getting, Keeping & Working With Your Acting Agent*, it is still, nevertheless, a vital and important part of the relationship.

An agent does not sign talent for fun. They sign talent they believe in and whom they think they can build a career for (and with). It is not in an agent's interest to sign talent they do not think they can make money with (and for). Most agents hope, therefore, that the relationship will be not just successful and lucrative, but also long-lasting.

When agents take on a client, they believe they are taking them on for the long haul. Otherwise what's the point in doing it? We have to believe we see an extraordinary talent in you and we trust in our own ability as an agent to be the person who nurtures and develops that talent, and takes it to the heights it is capable of reaching. This is true for most agents. We are taking you on because we believe in you, we believe in ourselves, and we believe in the best possible outcome for us working together. A good agent works with you to help develop a productive and prosperous career; a great agent sees potential in you that you don't even see in yourself – and the best agents help you to believe in it.

Having said that, what happens if and when you get to the point that you think it is time to move on? And what does it mean if your agent lets you go?

One of the main reasons for moving on from an agent is because it has been quiet in terms of auditioning for a sustained period of time. In these cases, it is important to remember that building a relationship takes time. The relationship isn't always perfect straight off the bat, the auditions aren't all immediately ideal, you're not always booking every job you go in for. Look first at the length of time you've been with your agent. If it's been less than a year, and unless things are absolutely dreadful and the relationship has irrevocably broken down, it would be prudent to wait a little longer.

In most instances, it takes a few months for things to settle down and bed in. Your agent is working hard for you from the moment they sign you, but it can take time for potential employers to want to see you. During this time, your agent is building up a picture of how the industry sees you, and working out how they can market you and your unique skills in order to make you stand out in an overcrowded profession. During these first few months of the relationship, your agent is also learning about you. Of course, they hope that they can get you out working as quickly as possible in a job that makes you happy. The sooner you are booking jobs, the sooner your agent is earning money.

The industry is cyclical, though. It is not frenetically busy all year round. Like all industries, there are busy periods and quiet periods. When you sign with your agent, how busy you are and how soon will depend on what time of year it is. July, August and September are typically quieter months in the industry. There seems to be a natural ebb and flow around the school holidays. Agencies can also be very quiet in the run-up to, and the period just after, Christmas, and so on. If you sign with an agent over the summer, in late November or early December, it can take a little longer before you see results as there's not as much work being cast.

How busy you are also depends on events happening in the world. Nobody could have expected that in 2020 the entire industry would completely shut down due to a global pandemic. We could not have anticipated that, nor could we have anticipated the effect the shutdown would have on the industry – and the impact it will continue to have over subsequent years. When the economy is quiet and contracting and we're in an age of recession or austerity, there is less work around for everyone. The big film star starts taking on TV roles. The TV star takes on theatre roles. And the theatre actor takes on fringe productions. Sadly, that leaves nowhere for actors starting out on the fringe to go.

Devastatingly, a lot of venues and companies closed for good during the pandemic. Regional theatres would once have employed thousands of actors a year, and without that ecosystem there is generally less work available. In such times, everybody struggles to make a living, with more performers out of work and available, and more choice for employers from an already-overcrowded talent pool.

There are any number of reasons why it might be quiet for you and why you might be thinking about leaving your agent. Perhaps you feel you're not getting seen for the right stuff; you don't feel comfortable talking to your agent; you feel you have been forgotten or you are no onger a priority; you wonder whether you have chosen the right agent or you doubt that the fit is correct.

Whilst it may sound like passing the buck, before automatically assuming your agent is not working hard for you, ask yourself if you are working hard for yourself. An agent is trying to sell your package; if no one is buying, the first step is to look at the marketing materials – an honest interrogation of your own CV, headshot and showreel should be the first port of call. Is everything up to date? Is your headshot clear, detailed and professional? Are your credits easy to understand and focused on the type of work you want to be doing? Are you trying to push yourself for TV and film work with no showreel or evidence of working in screen or training in that field? Just because you've completed a three-year course in musical theatre does not necessarily mean you will automatically be seen for TV, film or 'straight' theatre. Your CV is a record of the field you have been working in most, and it is reasonable for the industry to assume that this is the technique, genre or style in which you are strongest.

Talk to your agent about this. They should be advising you on how to make your CV appeal to casting directors and how to shape it to cater to your desires. Your agent may also have ideas about training courses you could take, or advise you on how much competition there is in your casting bracket. It is unfortunate that the 20- to 30-year-old age bracket is the most oversubscribed in the industry, so it is not surprising that many actors in this bracket change agents frequently.

Wherever you go, however, you take yourself with you. If the problem is with your CV, then a new agent will not effect much change without your help in understanding and addressing the issues.

Sometimes you may want to move on because you feel there is a lack of communication with your agent. It can seem easier to move on than to address the issue. Explain to your agent that you need a more open and accessible line of communication, that you want the type of relationship where you can pick up the phone and have a chat with them about something. Discuss your needs and find out about their boundaries in this area. How much communication you need not only varies from actor to actor but also varies from year to year. An actor having a quiet period usually needs more reassurance from their agent than an actor who is in consistent work.

The first stage should *always* be to talk to your agent. This is your career, your journey, and your own personal relationship with your agent. Talk to them, work out a way of communicating and see if there is a possibility of improving the relationship. If you do not feel comfortable doing that, if that scares you or you feel it is impossible then perhaps you are, indeed, with the wrong agent. If that's not the case, drop your agent an email, explain you have some things you'd like to discuss, and make an appointment. A chat with your agent will usually throw up some interesting ideas both for you *and* your agent. Your agent may not know that you are unhappy with the types of jobs for which you are being submitted. Your lack of interest in the castings they are arranging may be causing you to be lacking in energy in the audition room. Usually, a chat will clear the air and get you back on the same page.

It happens that lot of time can go past when you and your agent don't see each other. It is surprising how quickly you can change physically. If that is the case, it is worth asking for a face-to-face meeting rather than a phone call. Ask to drop by, so they can see what you look like on a day-to-day basis rather than how you look in a headshot which may be out of date. Agents work a lot from headshots, looking at the same pictures over and over hundreds of times in a day. They can get a little bit obsessed with how clients look in a headshot. When was your headshot last updated? Do you still look the same?

If you have been using the same headshot for a very long time it can get to the point where 'headshot fatigue' has set in. A casting director will see you being submitted for far more jobs than you are being called in for. Changing the headshot can sometimes really jolt a casting director into taking a second look at you. This is particularly important if you have changed your look, cut your hair, lost or gained some weight. If this is the case, let your agent know.

A casting director often only has your headshot to go on when deciding to call you in, and you may have been asked in because you fit a certain look. It is essential that the person they are expecting is the one who comes in the door. No one particularly cares how old you look, or what you look like in general; what matters is that you look as expected. A casting director may call you in because they remember meeting you before, or seeing your showcase or graduation show a year ago. Your headshot should reflect your current look or you may be wasting the casting director's time.

At some stage in your career you may feel it is time to 'move up'. You may feel you have reached a point where you have acquired some profile and you want to take your career to the next level. Usually when an actor has acquired this kind of profile they may well have had some approaches from bigger agencies. As your profile grows, bigger agencies take notice. These agencies need a lot of big-money clients; they handle big careers. There is a lot to be said for the confidence boost of being with the same international agent as Academy Award winners. With big agencies there is a lot of 'big' information and the network of professionals a big agency works with may be considerably larger. A big agency will certainly be seeing more casting breakdowns, and so there may be more doors opened and more opportunity for the actor. Working with 'big' careers can mean 'big' money too, and the negotiating clout of a big agency can be considerable. The move 'up' is not always without its pressures and its pitfalls, however.

With a big agency comes an expectation that you will be a big client and you will *remain* a big client. That can put considerable pressure on you and your work. It may well take a period of adjustment. Many actors who spend their early years moving happily from job to job, rarely out of work and busy all the time, suddenly find themselves on the lucky end of that 'big break' and move to a big agency.

At this point, the constant work may stop. Many big agencies have their own ideas about what kind of work you should be doing at this level. You may go from being the most well-known name up for a project to being in a room full of major industry players with awards and accolades longer than your arm. It is likely that you will also now go from being a big earner for your agency and thus receiving a lot of care and attention, to being one in amongst a much larger pool. The expectation for you to demonstrate your worth can feel overwhelming and, in some cases, it may be coupled with reduced individual attention. As with everything, consider what you are prepared to sacrifice in order to achieve what you wish to achieve.

You may, after a time, feel you need to move sideways for a different focus. Perhaps your agent has a speciality, a particular focus, or seems to have a lot of contacts in an area of interest that you don't work in any more. Perhaps you never did work in that field or perhaps your own interest has shifted.

Agents are always learning and developing too – and maybe their interests and focus have shifted. Perhaps you want to work in an area where you don't feel your agent has the right skill set and contact book to enable this. If this is the case, you may want to move sideways to an agent who has a focus on, or seems stronger in, a particular area. If this is why you want to move it is worth remembering that the move alone will not change your CV. You will need to put in the work yourself on demonstrating your ability and proficiency in that area.

You may simply want to move agents to get a fresh perspective. There is an old saying, 'Familiarity breeds contempt' – but perhaps it should be 'Familiarity breeds contentment'. We can become complacent, too comfortable, too relaxed about things if we stay in the same place for too long. I think that creatives often need change and excitement to do their best work. Being slightly out of your comfort zone can re-energise you. Sometimes you just need to get things moving again. If you want something to change, change something.

Whatever your reasons for wanting to move on, the most essential component of your relationship with your agent is communication. Nine times out of ten, an agent already knows when a client is thinking of leaving. Perhaps it's a special 'agent's sense'. Whatever it is, they usually suspect – *so talk to them.*

Possibly they have a completely different idea of what work you are interested in because they signed you a year or two ago and they are still thinking of you in that way. You can develop and change a lot, and any problems might be solved by having a chat, readjusting expectations on both sides, and agreeing to try a new approach.

If it is quiet for your career, then your career is quiet for your agent, and they will have noticed. They may also have been thinking about letting you go because they haven't been able to do as much for you and they are just as worried as you are about how to broach the subject. Whatever the situation, you will feel better about it if you are open and honest.

Your agent is a human being and breaking up with them is painful on both sides. Whether you are saying 'I don't think this is working out and I want to try someone else', or you are saying 'I've been offered representation at a big agency', it is hard to hear. Your agent has put a lot of time, thought and investment into you. They work for you in the hope and belief that one day they will earn commission from your career. It can be very hurtful to be told you haven't done enough. However, it is a business relationship and that means it must be a business relationship on both sides.

Do not, however tempted you may be, burn any bridges. You never know when you're going to need that person. Agents often move around themselves. You never know when the agent that you've left behind may themselves move to a new agency or become the next big thing. Leave the relationship with your – and their – dignity intact. Be respectful, acknowledge the time and the energy they put in for you, and thank them. Be a professional and be an adult.

Being let go by your agent is often talked of as being the worst thing that can happen. The euphemisms used – being dumped, being dropped, being let go – all contribute to the emotional upheaval and feeling of free-falling without support.

So much of what creatives do is tied to our perception of who we are as human beings. What we do is who we are. When an actor, or a creative, presents themselves at an audition or in a performance and is rejected, it can feel like it is *them* as a human that is being rejected. It is important to remember that this is not the case.

Creatives are intrinsically linked with their creative output. It is their heart and soul, the essence of who they are. Being let go by an agent can feel like the world has ended. It is bewildering and painful. It can affect your confidence and make you question yourself. As much as it's a cliché to say that everything is a learning experience, it is still, nonetheless, true. Everything is growth. Growth is painful, but growth is also necessary. Momentum is good. Stay positive and see opportunity.

If you're being let go, there are any number of reasons why. If your agent is one agent in a larger company, the instruction may have come from higher up; an agency is a business and your agent needs to cover their overheads. Perhaps someone higher up in the company has gone through their client list and identified clients who are not earning as much money as they could. Letting go of some clients can free up space on an agent's list to bring in some new talent.

Your agent may be moving to another agency or leaving the company to set up their own agency or retiring from the industry. In many cases, the old agency will try to keep as many clients as possible and redistribute them to other agents, but there may simply be too many clients to hold on to all of them. If your agent is leaving they may have signed a severance agreement prohibiting them from talking to you for a number of months. It can seem like they've just abandoned you, but it may simply be they are contractually prevented from contacting you.

Your agent may let you go because they feel they have been unable to open the right doors for you. The aim of the actor–agent relationship is a productive, working association. It is not helpful to you, or to your agent, to have you sitting on their books doing nothing.

Occasionally, with the best will in the world, an agent is unable, for whatever reason, to be able to get you through the doors. For the good of your career, there comes a time when an agent might admit defeat and encourage you to find new representation to help you get the career you deserve. Remember, they sign you because they believe in you and your talent. If they have been unable to help you then they are holding you back. Letting you go may well be the best thing for your career.

Agents do this job because they love it, but, at the end of the day, it's a job and they have certain expectations of the people they work with. In some, very rare, situations you may be let go because you are not fulfilling your part of the contract. If you are constantly ill-prepared, if you're constantly late, if you're constantly rude or arrogant or difficult, if you are constantly cancelling or letting people down, then you are not only making yourself look bad, but it is reflecting on your agent and thus reflecting on the rest of the client list. Your agent has a duty to protect the agency's reputation for the sake of all the clients.

There may be myriad reasons why you are underprepared, why you are late, why you are struggling. Communicating with your agent about what is happening in your life, how auditions are going and what difficulties you may be having is essential. If your behaviour is causing problems then talking to your agent about any difficulties you are having could make things so much better for you. Human beings first, actors second, remember?

Many agencies have a clause in your contract about personal behaviour. If you are behaving badly on set or in rehearsal, or if you make statements on your social media that are ncompatible with the beliefs and ethos of your agent, that are potentially damaging and bringing the agency or your agent into disrepute, they may invoke this clause.

Momentum is a good thing, but that doesn't mean changing your agent every three or four months. This is an industry that values loyalty and reputation. No one expects blind loyalty, of course, but the industry likes people that are dependable and respectful. Momentum doesn't mean moving around, and moving on to somebody new, or moving up, down or sideways; it means constantly being in communication with your agent, continually developing as an actor, moving and changing with the industry. Your agent can be there to guide you on trends they're seeing and encourage you to develop, train and start meeting people in those fields. Your agent can help you keep moving, keep your momentum going.

Finally, when moving on, make sure you understand how the contract with your agent works. If you are on a job, your agent will continue to receive the commission from that job. If you have just booked the lead in a big West End musical and signed a year's contract then, in most cases, your old agent will continue to handle the contract and you will continue to pay them their commission.

Make sure you fully understand the agreement you have signed, as the agreement is between you and your old agent, not between your old agent and your new one. You may find yourself paying commission to two agents if you are not completely clear on the terms of the contract. Some agents might buy somebody out of their contract, but that's rarer than you might expect.

Check your contract before you give notice to see what the notice period is. This can vary depending on the agency. Some agents have notice periods of one month, some three months, some even expect notice periods of six months. You could find yourself, having told your agent you want to leave, sat on their books for six months. One hopes that during those six months they continue to submit you for work and make every best effort to secure work for you. Meanwhile, your new agent is twiddling their thumbs waiting for you – and you're hoping they're still as excited about you in six months' time.

The Personal Managers' Association takes the position that, once a client no longer wishes to be represented by an agency, the agency no longer has the right to represent that client. If your agent is a member of the PMA and does not adhere to this guideline it is worth asking them why. Happily, that's a worst-case scenario. In many cases, an agent will, regardless of how long the contractual notice period is, let you go almost immediately. If you have expressed the desire to leave and if the relationship has broken down irrevocably to the point where you need to go, then few agents would want to keep you tied to them.

There is no hard-and-fast rule for the best way to break up with your agent. Some agents prefer to hear the final news via email, but others may prefer a call. An email allows your agent to process the news in their own time. A telephone call or a face-to-face meeting only allows for an immediate reaction which can be unpredictable – shock, surprise, anger, tears. It is better to leave your agent to have their reaction in private. You may want to continue to have a personal relationship with your agent after leaving. Like any break-up, it's probably best to give it some time before you try this.

3. Working With...

Working in this industry is hard. You'll have heard that quite a few times already. From the very first time we articulate the idea that we might like to work in the creative industry, most of us will encounter tremendous opposition. My father worked in this industry, but even so, when I told my parents I wanted to go to drama school, not university, the response was a resounding 'No chance'.

'It's hard!' 'It's the hardest career in the world.' 'You can't make any money out of it.' 'You'll never get anywhere.' 'Why would you want to spend your life messing around like that?'...

A wall of well-meaning dissuasion. Ultimately, it is utterly pointless. Once the bug has bitten you, it's practically impossible to ignore the itch.

What you need to know is not how hard it is, but how it can be easier. And believe it or not, it *can* be easier. In this chapter I will look at some strategies to help you feel a bit more in control of your career, some ways of working with your agent so that the relationship is more balanced, and some techniques that could be beneficial to you in the long run.

The industry is hard, yes, but it doesn't have to be impossible. It doesn't have to drain the life-force out of you. You don't have to move into a garret and subsist on a diet of cold baked beans and regret. Your self-esteem does not have to be in the toilet, and you don't have to avoid family gatherings. It is possible to live a fulfilled and creative life despite the paucity of work, the lack of opportunity, and the relentless, exhausting marathon of pursuing your dreams. You will need tenacity, endurance and optimism, a commitment to a disciplined process, and an unshakeable belief in the maxim that anything worth having is worth working for.

Working

The primary objective of the actor–agent relationship is to get work, so it would be reductive to have a chapter about working with your agent without actually talking about what happens when you get it.

At some point, hopefully sooner rather than later, you will be offered a job. You will, of course, be delighted and itching to get started, but it is a useful practice to develop a habit of discussing with your agent the pros and cons of any particular job. In this way you will learn a little about the industry and begin to appreciate how your work is viewed. It is worth speaking to your agent and asking what they know about the company, where the show is touring, the size of the venues, how this particular job may benefit you or work against you in terms of building a career. It is always worth having a conversation with your agent about the calibre of the job you are being offered.

A good way to think about work is to ask yourself whether it falls into the category of work you're doing for cash, work you're doing for kudos, or work you're doing for kicks. The dream job, hopefully, is one that fulfils all those needs – and more besides. In an ideal world, every job would bring you creative fulfilment, the respect of your friends, family and peers, and the money to pay the bills. Sadly, not every job is a dream job.

Every job will, hopefully, hit at least one of these, but understanding why you're taking a job will help you feel more comfortable and more balanced if it fails to be completely perfect.

Are you doing it for *cash*? Do you need to make rent, pay bills, get new headshots, renew Spotlight? There's many a job taken just for the cash – don't be ashamed of taking a job because you need money. One day, every job ends up being just another line on a CV.

Are you doing it for *kudos*? Are you doing it because the director has profile, or the venue, or the writer, or the other actors involved? Are you working with people at the top of their game, who will really stretch you? Remember it's often not the size of the part that matters, but what it demonstrates about you as an actor – the company you keep, the choices you make. Are you forward-thinking?

Or are you doing it for *kicks*? It's called a 'play' for a reason. There are many jobs that, on the surface, would seem to have little going for them other than to be doing something, to feel like an actor again. It may be a job with good friends that you know will be fun; it may be a terrific part that you know will teach you something about your process; it may fill some time in between other jobs or alleviate the boredom of your day job. Sometimes the jobs we do for fun turn out to be the most rewarding, opening up avenues we may never have considered before.

Knowing why you have decided to take a particular job, and developing the critical practice to assess your choices throughout your career, is very useful. There are many big Hollywood stars who advocate the mantra of 'One for them, one for me' – one job for their fans, or the money, or the profile, followed by one job that's just for them, a little art-house film, a small indie project, a play... Build the career that *you* want, and keep a healthy balance between what the industry expects of you and what you expect of yourself.

Whatever the job, remember that a contract is a legal agreement. Once you have signed you are obligated and committed to complete the work you have agreed to do. You should not, therefore, sign a contract without understanding it and without considering all the ramifications that a legally binding document constitutes.

Sometimes the negotiations on a contract may take a while and it's unlikely that your agent will check in with you every step of the way. They are working hard to get the best deal for you, which will include negotiating your fee, and ensuring you are protected and supported. Depending on the production, and on your own status and profile, these negotiations could take some time. Do make sure, if you have specific questions or requirements, that you raise these early so your agent is negotiating with a full deck of cards. It can be very frustrating for you, for the agent, and for the production if the contract is all but agreed before you remember you need two days off in the middle of shooting to attend a wedding. Your agent is there to advise you on what is a reasonable request and then to be your representation in getting you the best possible deal.

When you are working, your agent will be supporting you in a variety of ways. A primary role of the agent is to take the pressure off you, so you can focus on doing your best, most creative work. An agent is therefore the person you need to speak to about any difficulties you may be having – whether that's to raise concerns about how you are being treated in rehearsal or to complain that the waste bin in your trailer is never emptied. It is useful to have an agent to fight your battles for you so that your working relationships with the director or production team aren't compromised by any external difficulties you may be having.

During the run of a show, your agent will be doing their best to bring industry professionals to see you work. They will almost certainly attend your first night, collate your reviews and promote your work. They may visit you on set, assist you with press junkets, and will be your advocate in meetings. The busier you are, the more there is for your agent to do, and so the relationship should be flexible and versatile. Some agents are more 'full service' than others, but most usually play some variation of a personal manager's role.

Planning Your Career

One of the great joys of being an agent is helping clients with their career development. If the term 'development' suggests a straightforward direction, then first you need to be reminded once more that you are individual and unique.

The quality of individuality everyone constantly suggests you try to find is also a vital component for developing your career. Your journey is unique to you, the path you take is your own particular path, the obstacles you encounter are particular to your journey, and the time it takes is specific to you and you alone.

There is no one you are in competition with, no race you need to win, no comparison that is relevant or appropriate. This journey is all your own. It is not a mountain to climb, but a mountain range to explore. Whenever you have climbed one particular mountain, rest assured that, as soon as you scale the peak, there will be another one. And whatever plans you might have, understand that the universe has some plans of its own.

Many drama schools, as part of the assessment criteria of the course, guide students to write five-year plans. In an industry as capricious and uncertain as ours you'd be forgiven for thinking that planning is pointless. Actually, plans can very useful tools, but perhaps a better name for five-year plans might be 'five-year dreams'.

A plan is a dream written down, so dream as big, as wide and as bravely as possible, for as long as possible. When you have dreamed your biggest, when you have really allowed yourself to dream without inhibition or fear, write that dream down. That is a goal. It is not *the* goal, nor should it be your only goal. Maybe it's your Monday goal and on Tuesday you have another one, equally big, equally wild, equally brave. Have another on Wednesday, and so on.

This advice may well be in direct contrast to everything you have ever been told about this industry. You may have been told you need to focus, focus, focus, to have one goal and pursue it relentlessly and endlessly until you achieve it. You may have heard you need to discover your one true purpose and then hone in or you'll never be happy. How has that been working out?

Most of us have a number of ambitions. What are yours?

- 'I want to be in a West End musical.'
- 'I want to be a regular in a soap opera.'
- 'I'd like to try a bit of everything.'
- 'I want to see my name on the credits of a major feature film.'
- 'I want to write a play.'

And so on, and so on.

Depending on what stage of your career you are currently at, these ambitions may seem unobtainable or they may seem within your grasp. The interesting question is usually, 'What happens after?' Imagine you spent your entire life focused on the first of those – to be in a West End musical. What happens if you spent twenty years of your career working towards it and finally achieve it at the age of 35? What's next? Another West End musical? Fantastic, but then your ambition isn't 'to be in a West End musical', but 'to have a sustained and lasting career in West End musicals'.

That's a bigger, wilder, braver dream. The skill set you need for that dream is different to the skill set you'll need for the other dream. One involves developing the stamina, skills, mental discipline and versatility to go from show to show to show. The other involves developing the skill set for one particular role in one specific show.

'What happens next?' is a crucial question to ask yourself in order to truly work out your ambitions. A lot of five-year plans work forwards and are time-limited. They work on the assumption that one thing leads to another. In this industry, as in life, this is rarely the case.

Life is not predictable or logical, and nor is this career. One of the definitions of 'career' is the noun – 'An occupation undertaken for a significant period of a person's life and with opportunities for progress' – but in our industry, the more useful definition is the verb – 'To move swiftly and in an uncontrolled way.' You can plan to go from A to Z, but that still takes in twenty-four other letters along the way. Working from the assumption that one thing leads to another isn't helpful.

A more useful tool for career planning is 'backwards planning'. Have a detailed, specific and huge end goal in mind, work out how you'd get there, and then begin moving in that direction.

One of the most versatile and admirable careers of anyone in this industry is that of Dame Judi Dench. At 86 years old, at time of writing, she has had an enviable career. Imagine if, aged 86, Dame Judi decided to call it quits. Most actors would be extremely grateful to get to that age still doing what they love. I think we can safely assume she has 'made it'. An icon, a national treasure, universally revered, critically respected, adored by colleagues and audiences, as an actor she is known all over the world… By any definition of 'making it', Dame Judi must rank pretty highly.

Let's put that on a chart and take a look. Of course, Dame Judi's career hasn't been a straight line, far from it. There have been ups and downs and roundabouts all over the place. But there she is, 86 years old and at the top of her game.

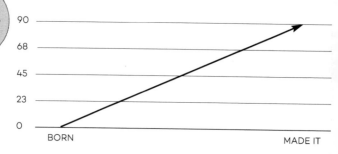

Where are you on that chart? How far into your own journey are you? Wherever you sit on this crude trajectory, you still have so much left to do and, whilst that's probably an exhausting thought, it is also an exhilarating one.

Here's another way of looking at it. One of the most beloved TV series of the last half-century was *Friends*. It ran for ten seasons and two hundred and thirty-six episodes. An entire generation grew up with those characters and they grew up in front of us. If your life was *Friends*, what season would you be in? Are you heading towards the cliffhanger of Season One: 'The One Where Rachel Finds Out'? Or are you midway through Season Five: 'The One Where Everybody Finds Out'? Are you maybe in a mid-season hiatus? Perhaps the writers are on strike? You may feel like you've been written out. Don't worry – how many times did Janice come back? Wherever you are on your journey, there's more to come. More twists and turns, more cliffhangers, more plot holes, more dead ends, more break-ups, and more happiness.

Let's say you want to 'do it all'. Let's say you want to reach the age of 86 and look back. That is truly the biggest, wildest, bravest dream. But that's exactly where we should begin: with the biggest, boldest, widest, bravest dream imaginable.

Draw a pyramid and write that dream at the top. Now work backwards; look at the step just beneath it. Let's say the big dream is that you want to win awards for your acting, like Dench; the step right before that would be 'Be in roles that get me nominated for awards', right? There's literally no other way of achieving your goal, is there? So that's the step immediately before achieving it.

The Big Dream!

What needs to happen just before that? 'Successfully audition for the role' would be a good step. And before that? 'Have the type of career that gives me the opportunity to meet the people that will audition me for those roles' – how's that? And before that? 'Build a CV of great work' or 'Create work that gets me noticed', and so on, step by step by step, right back to where you are right now.

It may be that one of those steps is 'Get signed by a top agent' or 'Graduate top of my class from a leading drama school'; each step is going to be particular to you. 'Get very lucky' is not a step, sadly. Sure, it might happen, but you can't plan for it – you can't rely on luck. All you can rely on is your own process and preparation.

Climbing a pyramid on your own is hard work. If you have a team helping you – a wide base of contacts and collaborators and a vast network – then the climb is easier.

A favourite saying of mine is 'You can't jump the Grand Canyon on a unicycle.' You can't bypass all the necessary steps. You can't win an Academy Award until you're nominated for one. You can't land an Academy Award-eligible role until you've been seen by the right people. You can't be seen by the right people until you've taken the steps leading up to that.

This is the process. We all want to rush process, we're all looking at ways to speed on through, to try and jump the Grand Canyon before we're ready. That is human nature. We live in a fast-moving world and we want things fast. Faster now than we have ever wanted them before.

You'll get there a whole lot faster if you put the work in. Practise process. It's the journey that's exciting, not the destination. Always be learning, always be travelling, always be working along your own path. The only person timing your journey is you. Give yourself a break.

Just as the most valuable resource an agent has is their clients, the most valuable resource an actor has is their contacts. Many actors spend a lot of time following the careers of other actors. That can breed resentment. Instead, follow ASMs, DSMs, ADs and casting assistants – those are the people in whom you should invest your energy. They'll be maturing and developing at the same time as you. Today's casting assistant is tomorrow's Head of Casting at the National Theatre. Everyone, *everyone*, working in this industry is of value to everyone else.

Don't limit your contacts list to people. Thanks to Twitter, you can build relationships with venues too. Tweet the venues of work you've enjoyed. Who knows, the artistic director may retweet you, or at least like your tweet, and you can start to develop a relationship there. People want to work with people who are invested in them, and in their work. Demonstrate your interest and investment.

Get out. Go to as many press nights as you can – particularly if you have friends in the show. See if you can meet the creative team, compliment them on their work, talk to them about their upcoming projects. Keep your notebook on you at all times and write down anything you remember. It will show you to be informed and interested when you write to them later.

Going to press nights is expensive, but those aren't the only places to meet people. Casting directors don't always get tickets for press nights (particularly for the big shows), but they might go to the first preview. Don't forget, when you've seen something you enjoyed, to say 'Thank you'! Tweet the casting director and compliment them. A little flattery goes a long way. Don't overdo it, though; just enough to keep in touch. And remember – the casting director is part of a larger puzzle, so start building your network of up-and-coming creatives, not just casting directors.

The rapper Genesis Elijah recommends that you 'Build your base wide before you build high.' The pyramids at Giza have stood this long precisely because they obey this rule. Their wide base gives them solidity and structure to survive generations. They were built to last. Build your own base wide, make your network as diverse and solid as you can, and you will build a structure that lasts.

As your network builds, share this information with your agent. Let them know with whom you have been meeting, chatting or building relationships. It can really help your agent when they are talking you up to a casting director if they are able to mention that the casting director has already met you at a workshop or via email.

Checking In

The longer you are with your agent, the easier it is to forget to check in. One simply assumes that everything is going well and you don't need to be in touch with them. It is incumbent upon the agent to check in with the client, but you should remember to check in with your agent too. You are working with someone who has their own life, their own personal relationships, and their own things happening. If you expect them to be interested in you, be interested in them. When you drop them a line to let them know what you've been up to or how *your* life is going, remember to check in on *them* at the same time.

When a client is on a long job, agents usually only hear from them if there's a problem. If a client is happy, they rarely have the need to get in touch with their agent.

Agents love their clients being happy, we love knowing you are out there enjoying your work and enjoying being creative. Agents can keep up with most of their clients via their social media and we love seeing you enjoying your life because that is what this industry should be about – living a happy, creative life that expands beyond the job you are engaged in.

Even in a long job, though, it's important to keep your agent informed about what's happening. How you feel about the job may change. You may find yourself losing your love for it. There may be difficulties in the cast or the company. It is not unusual, once the initial elation has worn off, for a long contract to lose its lustre. Your agent has usually been through this situation with dozens of other clients and can talk you through what to expect.

It is also useful to keep your agent up to date on any news you hear. Sharing information with your agent is important. As an actor, you are out there working, socialising, meeting other people, hearing all the gossip. It's interesting for agents to share news with you and for us to hear your news, to hear about what you are spending your time on when you're not performing. Nurture the relationship and give it attention, so it can grow and bloom and become the beautiful orchard you require it to be, bearing fruit for both of you for years to come.

Managing Your Mental Health

In managing your relationship with your agent, it is vitally important to have a healthy understanding of mental health in the industry. A 2015 survey from the University of Victoria in Australia recorded that creative workers in the performing arts are ten times more likely than the general population to have mental-health issues.

When you think about the uncertainty of the profession – the constant rejection, the periods of unemployment, the knockbacks, the blows to self-esteem, not to mention the continual moving around and uprooting to travel for work – it is no wonder the figures are so high (and likely to be rising since the pandemic). Anxiety is one of the most prevalent issues we currently see in the industry, and impacts everyone in the creative arts: performers, composers, musical directors, directors, producers, agents – every single person you work with in this industry is at high risk of mental-health issues. It's a positive thing to have a healthy understanding and relationship with your mental health, and this includes the ability to speak to your agent, who hopefully is sensitive and understanding.

If you're suffering, if you try to block any conversation about it, or pretend that it's not happening, there is a danger that you will harm your relationship with your agent. Your agent will continue to push you out for auditions – if you're not feeling ready to be going out to auditions, this can cause problems and lead to a breakdown in the relationship. If your agent isn't aware of what's going on, they may worry that you are not committed to your work. Keep an open communication with your agent about what you're going through.

It can sometimes feel like there is a hierarchical imbalance in the industry that prevents us from talking about problems we are having. Actors sometimes worry whether being open about struggling, physically or mentally, might affect how the industry perceives them. There may also be a fear that admitting to struggling may seem disingenuous if a career is, superficially at least, 'going well'. It is very important to have somebody you feel is on your side, someone to talk to who can guide you through these periods. Help is available if we know where to look and how to reach for it.

There are a lot of services out there that can provide you with the assistance you need to make sure that you are working in a healthy and happy way, and you're taking care of yourself. The industry can often focus too much on physical health, and neglect to focus on mental health. We need to look after and look out for one another.

There are a number of industry-specific websites you can access, and organisations you can speak to, but being able to talk to your agent is vital; it's probably the most fundamentally important relationship that you'll have within the industry. Agents should be able to direct you to talking therapies, and to useful resources that can help and assist you. If they do not have personal experience then they will usually have worked with someone who has. Your agent has experience and knowledge – don't be afraid to avail yourself of it. Being able to take the pressure off yourself, and knowing you are with an agent who understands how difficult it is to be out there, putting yourself on display and being open to rejection and criticism every day of your working life, can be a relief in itself.

Resting

At some point in your acting career, there will be downtime. Traditionally this downtime is called 'resting' and it is called that for a reason. To build a long-lasting and strong physical body we need to rest in between periods of exercise. The same applies to building a long-lasting and strong creative mindset.

Resting is necessary. It rejuvenates the body, the mind and the soul. A lot of actors would have you believe that in order to be a successful actor you need to go from job to job to job to job to job – to keep working continuously.

Whilst it is wonderful if you can manage to keep working, it is actually very rare and not necessarily something to which you should aspire. Sometimes, the mistaken belief that you have to keep working leads to you burning yourself out on work of inconsistent quality. It's easier to stay in work if you're indiscriminate about the quality, and even easier if you're not being paid for the work you do.

Work begets work – and the same type of work. The more you work for free, the more people will ask you to work for free. There is nothing wrong with working for free on a project you care passionately about, but as a professional you should value yourself enough to be paid. A very good reason to work for free on something is if it is your own work.

At some points in your career, you're going to have periods of resting, of not working. It is useful to think of the times when you are employed as being the times you're on holiday! When you're in a job, it hopefully shouldn't feel like a job. You're being paid to do what you love, you can relax, enjoy the boost to your self-confidence, kick back and revel in it all.

It's when you're out of a job that the hard work actually begins. This is when the real job of acting begins – back to the 'day job', back to the grind of the audition room, back to the merry-go-round of rejection. Your relationship with your agent should not change whilst you are resting. You should continue to carve out time to check in with them, update them on the classes you are taking, the people you are writing to, the meetings you are having. A useful question at this point is always 'What can I be doing to help?' This encourages you to work collaboratively with your agent and to make sure that both of you are still moving the train in the right direction. It is, however, important to remember that it is called 'resting' for a reason. It is a useful time to recharge your batteries and take stock of where you are, to reflect on the experience you have just had. This is also usually the time you will hear a lot about creating your own work.

Creating Your Own Work

In almost every acting seminar at some point 'creating your own work' will come up. When you are advised to create your own work, it doesn't necessarily mean you need to make a film, put on a show, organise a tour, take something to the Edinburgh Fringe or produce a cabaret. They are all excellent examples of making your own work, but they are all pretty far down the line of doing so. Making your own work means *leaning in* to what you love to do.

Actors are storytellers, essentially. It is in your DNA, a tradition that goes back thousands of years. You mostly tell other people's stories; sometimes you tell your own. Leaning in to what you love to do means examining the stories you are drawn to telling, and working out ways of telling more of them, to more people. Very few actors are business people, fewer still have the capability to tell stories at scale.

The first step of leaning in to what you love is to work out what story you want to tell. Like everything, this is a process. It is a journey not a destination. The aim is to develop your own creativity and, as such, it does not necessarily need an end result. If you produce anything, it will likely be very far from what you originally imagined. Making your own work is about the process and learning from that process. The path from A to Z goes through twenty-four other letters, remember? Well, the truth is that the path from A to Z goes through those twenty-four other letters and ends up at number six. Where you finish is rarely where you thought you would finish when you set out. Think of yourself as an explorer rather than a conqueror.

The goal of making your own work is to learn something about yourself, learn something about your own creativity and craft, and learn something about the discipline of being an out-of-work actor. Consider it part of your continued professional development and a continuation of your training, rather than a drive to get something finished and have a completed product at the end.

The instruction we began with in this book, as being one of the most fundamental building blocks of acting was 'Be Yourself.' Being yourself is a journey, it is not a destination. Creating your own work is one of the surest ways to learn about yourself. You will have to conquer your demons and triumph over them. You will have to learn how to sit comfortably with being incomplete. The idea that anything is complete, ever, is a myth.

If you were able to speak to the greatest artists in history, they would agree that, given the chance, they would go back and correct their mistakes and attempt to perfect the work. As you develop, so too does your artistry. Creating something will teach you to be always open to the idea of improvement.

Completion and perfection are the enemies of creativity. Making your own work will teach you the vital skill of embracing imperfection. As an actor, it is perhaps one of the most important skills you can learn: you will never be perfect. Learn to live with striving to be the best you can be.

Most of what you create will be imperfect. Experts will tell you that certain of Beethoven's symphonies are not as good as others. Symphony No. 2 is, for example, considered to be inferior to Symphony No. 3. But in order to get to Symphony No. 3, Beethoven had to go through the process of writing Symphony No. 2. Likewise, a lot of what you create will not be any good, but you are on your way to a masterpiece. 'Done' beats 'Perfect' every time.

Leaning in more to what you love means seizing every opportunity that comes your way; it means getting off the path you think you're on, ripping up the map you're following, and getting lost in the woods. It is about exploring your journey as a creative, rather than being fixed on a certain destination. Who knows what you might discover if you commit to following the path of what makes you happy. Focus on exploration not destination.

An actor acts. A writer writes. A director directs. But a creative? They create. If you can step back and see yourself as a 'creative' rather than an 'actor', you will open a world of possibility in your work. If you think of yourself as a creative whose job is to create, you are on the right path.

Creating your own work can be scary, which is why having mentors can be extremely valuable. Form your own Jedi Council. You can have real people, famous people, dead people, even imaginary people on your Jedi Council. There may be a fictional character you look up to. Imagine what they would say? What advice would they give? Make your Jedi Council as unique and individual to you as you can. Change up your Jedi Council whenever you need.

You may perhaps need to appoint somebody to whom you hold yourself accountable. Check in with them on fixed dates, when you have written a thousand words of your novel, when you have written the first three scenes of your play, when you have saved enough money to fund the short film. You may find your agent could be your checkpoint person, they may even be able to help or mentor you along the way. Remember that they have other clients, though, so even if they are willing to help, be respectful of their time and your demands on it.

Making your own work also has the additional benefit of creating a buzz around you – and people want to work with people who have a buzz around them. If there is a buzz around you in one area of your life or in one particular facet of your creativity, people tend to be a lot more adventurous in allowing you to explore other facets of your creativity. Use your buzz to open other doors.

Don't be afraid to collaborate. Don't be resistant to asking other people for help and to learning from them. Most art is, at some point, collaboration. Even when you write something entirely on your own, you will eventually hand that over to an editor, a dramaturg, a director, a designer, a producer or a creative, collaborative team who can bring your vision to life. Build your base wide, remember?

When creating your own work, recall the advice not to try to jump the Grand Canyon on a unicycle. Don't try to leap before you can run. Don't try to skip over steps, however tempting it may be. Why rush something you want to last forever? Learn, learn, learn all the time. All work is research. All work is beneficial. Take your time over your work and learn to enjoy the process.

We measure our achievement on a work–reward paradigm, and it is ingrained in us early. Hard work results in good SATs results. Then good GCSEs, good A levels, a good degree. We work hard and then we are rewarded with a piece of paper confirming that our hard work paid off.

But what happens after your degree? What happens in the real world? What happens when hard work gets you nowhere? Sadly, talent isn't enough, luck can't be guaranteed, and sometimes hard work leads us nowhere. A reward system that has been hard-wired into us over decades fails us. It can be dispiriting and disheartening and also incredibly expensive to keep working hard and not getting that reward – and too often we don't get the reward. We repeat the action and still don't get the reward.

The life of a creative involves being out of control quite a bit – there's so much we can't control. There are many reasons we don't have the success we crave as performers. We're doing everything right – why aren't we getting anywhere? Adjusting our thinking and enjoying the process is perhaps the greatest technique to ensure our longevity in this industry.

We need to believe that hard work is its own reward. Making your own work, doing something without expectation of a result, being creative just for the sake of it, and leaning in to what you love – this is the daily practice required to recalibrate the brain and to learn to love the process.

4. The Future

Having written over forty thousand words about where we are, I wanted to spend some time at the end of this book thinking about the future of the industry and where we might go next. Since I began writing this book in the spring of 2020 we have seen tremendous changes in the industry. We are going through a stage of restructuring, reorganising and reimagining our role in the community, and in society at large.

Studies demonstrate the average length of an actor's career is about two decades, and that most actors are only actively in work for about half of that time. Statistics you may have already heard or had pointed out to you show that only two per cent of actors earn over £50,000 a year, and ninety per cent of actors are out of work at any time.

The question is 'Why are you here?' Knowing how difficult the industry is, knowing how much struggle there is and how hard it is going to be, why are you still here? Theatres are closing at an alarming rate due to the coronavirus pandemic but, for some time now, there have not been enough theatres to cope with the volume of actors coming out of an increasing number of training courses. There are more opportunities for training, more schools and more courses than ever, but the number of opportunities to work in the industry has not increased proportionately.

We might look at the proliferation of web series, new streaming services like Netflix, Amazon Prime and Hulu, new technologies like motion capture and virtual reality, and conclude there must be lots of new opportunities for acting work – but still the number of opportunities does not match the number of actors coming in to the industry.

Where We Started

The history of acting has never been a path of security. Acting has never rated very highly on the scale of desirable professions. Whilst acting as a profession has been around for centuries, the meaning of the role changed over time. Being an actor in Ancient Greece, in the Middle Ages, at the dawn of the twentieth century or even in the 1950s, all meant very different things to what it means today. Actors in all of those periods would have had a very different understanding of what their career was.

Once upon a time, being an actor meant loading your belongings onto the back of a cart and spending your life moving around with a group of travelling players. You would perform your plays and poems and sing your songs in each town as you arrived. You would beg for scraps and the occasional warm bed to lay your head down. You would do it because you had stories to tell.

The Licensing Act of 1737 included actors who were not licensed by King George among the definitions of 'rogues and vagabonds':

> …every person who shall, for hire, gain or reward, act, represent or perform, or cause to be acted, represented or performed any interlude, tragedy, comedy, opera, play, farce or other entertainment of the stage, or any part or parts therein… shall be deemed to be a rogue and a

vagabond… and shall be liable and subject to all such penalties and punishments…

Acting was very much an art form for the people, for the proletariat. Professional actors didn't really begin to appear until the late thirteenth century, when monarchs would keep small companies of professional actors. Until the middle of the seventeenth century, there were only two patented theatre houses in England, and they were the only places where theatre could legally take place. Then came the Puritans, who viewed theatre as immoral, and closed the theatres down. It wasn't until the nineteenth century that acting started to become a profession that was admired in some places, with the first stars and celebrities emerging, and some actors forming their own companies. The rise of the actor-manager began. Still they would tour the country, performing for the people.

The hierarchical class system of acting we recognise now really didn't come into place until after the Industrial Revolution, when the middle classes began to attend theatre. Theatre has arguably remained, until recently, the sole preserve of the middle classes.

Where We Are

Theatre today is big business. Alongside the rise, over the last hundred years, of TV and film, theatre has helped create the modern star system and elevated actors to a position in society they had never held before. The profession continues to grow and, for some reason – despite continued dissuasion from families and careers advisers, despite increasing restrictions on funding, and against all statistics, the number of would-be actors entering the industry shows no signs of waning.

Why? Surely no one would deliberately choose to study and work towards a career with such demonstrably bad employment statistics? It is beyond sense and reason. In a society that values creativity as poorly as ours does, a society that exhausts itself trying to teach conformity rather than creativity, the fact that anyone would pursue a creative career must demonstrate that some of us are hooked on creativity early in our lives – and it is a habit we cannot shake.

There is a moment in our lives when we recognise our innate creativity, a moment we fall in love with it, and for creatives in all fields that tends to happen when we are very young. It is often a trigger event – a light-bulb moment – around the age of 5 or 6 years old. It is that first moment of being looked at, of making an audience laugh, of hearing the clarion sound of applause. Perhaps it is the first time our young brains are flooded with dopamine, the neurotransmitter which gives us that sweet sense of pleasure and reward, or the feeling of being part of a community, of fitting in, of being seen or heard for the first time. Most creatives have a memory of 'being creative' for the first time and, in almost all cases, it is a formative one.

Nobody talks about that moment as being when they realised they would one day be a world-famous, award-winning actor. It is more about connection with other people, born out of a sense of play. It can be a powerful memory to recall – the trigger memory – like the moment we fell in love for the first time. We spend most of our professional careers trying to recreate that moment, trying to get back to that feeling. In that sense it acts like a drug; perhaps this is why we have such a hard time quitting it.

Unfortunately, mainstream education does not nurture creativity. Education, as the late Sir Ken Robinson observed, does not teach us to grow *into* our creativity;

rather, it educates us out of it. In recent years, the idea that the purpose of education is to net us a high-paying job has become the prevailing ideology. Higher earners pay more income tax; low-earning creatives pay less. It serves the Treasury, HMRC and Capitalism to steer young minds away from creativity and towards productivity. We have devalued arts education and devalued creativity in such a way as to make it appear that it has no worth at all. Society tells us our value is linked to our monetary worth. Thus a 'good' job becomes a 'well-paid' job, regardless of whether it is artistically, emotionally or creatively fulfilling. Some people still slip through the net, however, ignoring the deterrents and pursuing their creative dreams – but because the continuous message is of how difficult it will be, the need to be successful becomes incredibly important. The definition of success has changed over the years.

Not long ago, an actor coming out of drama school would have felt themselves successful if they booked a role in rep or a Theatre-in-Education job. Any job that would help them along the route to getting their professional Equity card would have been seen as successful. Increasingly, those jobs have lost their kudos. The benchmark of success is constantly shifting, the bar repeatedly raised. Reaching the West End has become regarded as the pinnacle of a career. Some schools enforce this idea, some agents encourage it. Many actors pursue it, regardless of what their original ambitions were. It is certainly a fine ambition, but it is not everyone's ambition. And so we move further and further away from that light-bulb moment, from our initial desire simply to pursue a creative life.

The industry changed during the pandemic. The West End – that behemoth of the industry, in some ways and in some quarters – revealed itself as an emperor without any clothes. It was outdoor theatre that returned fastest. It was small-scale tours that brought theatre back to communities and gave actors their first jobs after the shutdown. Work that had been undervalued suddenly became sought after.

We need to adjust now, not only how we see ourselves as creatives, but how we define work that is 'good', 'valuable' or 'worthy'. We need to reconnect to our innate human need to express ourselves creatively.

Where We Are Going

Theatre has always been the backbone of the entertainment industry. Film joined the party from the turn of the twentieth century, with radio and TV joining the fold some two decades later. Since the 1920s, these four main pillars of the entertainment industry – theatre, film, radio, TV – have gone largely unchallenged. A career in the industry mainly meant working in one of these fields, crossover between them was unusual and remains difficult to this day. Theatre has usually been seen as the mother of them all, maintaining its allure and its stature; even huge Hollywood film stars speak with reverence of the credibility that theatre can bring to their careers.

All this is, however, changing, faster than you realise. Today, the world consumes content in a way that was unimaginable just a couple of decades ago. The rising talent of the industry is no longer likely to come from a solely theatrical training, if indeed they come from any training at all.

The agency of the future is already here. All signs point to a huge surge in agencies signing content creators. The big conglomerate agencies of America have long since diversified beyond TV, film and theatre. The race to sign the new, young, media-savvy content creators of TikTok and YouTube and the influencers of Instagram is where the big money deals are going.

Big talent comes with an already-existing following, in contrast to the stars who built their following *after* their fame. Where once big agencies turned to social media to build fan followings and commercial clout for their stars after their success, now that business model has shifted. Having an existing following comes first; the utilisation of that following and translating it to film and TV roles comes after.

The new generation of celebrity talent isn't sitting back and waiting for auditions to come to them; they're out there creating their own content, broadcasting it and distributing it on their own terms. They're used to fast results and are unwilling to be confined to one medium. Until relatively recently, social-media platforms were being used to move to a more traditional career – now the platform *is* the career. Digital is, to a whole generation, no longer an outpost of the talent industry – it *is* the industry. Brands are following them, big money is being spent on them, and the bigger the profile they have, the more opportunities come their way. The beauty blogger is signing TV contracts, the podcaster is writing scripts, the fashion influencer is creating content. Content is who we are, content is what we do, content is storytelling.

Agencies, meanwhile, always following the money, are bending the industry to suit this new way of working. The industry is going global in a manner never seen before and, as it does, many of the traditional methods of agenting are changing. Digital departments, influencer agents and digital-first careers are all fairly new additions to the infrastructure of an agency and, until recently, these departments were developing underground, outside of and away from the mainstream. Now the money diverted to these new departments is astronomical. Nurturing this new generation of talent and maximising opportunities for them is the new battleground for the industry.

The commission-based marketplace of the entertainment industry has always been a volatile one. The talent can, at any point, walk out the door. Agencies have always looked for alternative revenue streams. They have diversified into content creation, expanded beyond the traditional 'talent' into sports and media and events, and now they look to the digital world to expand their influence.

In many ways, though, agencies are merely playing catch-up to a new generation of talent who have already developed their own direct line of communication with an audience. The pandemic moved new media to the forefront like never before. Suddenly, online content, too often overlooked by the industry as a poor relation, became the sole way for creatives to continue creating. As we emerged from the lockdown, it seemed that the old quadrumvirate of theatre, radio, film and TV would stand tall once again, but the realisation that online content could be cheaper and quicker to produce continued to loom large.

The new world seemed to be more inclusive of new, more diverse voices and under-represented groups. The old ways began to look just that: old. Online content may still be the Wild West of the industry, but the opportunities are proliferating. Many creatives who shifted their output online found that it opened up more opportunities in the real world. Talent agents may have been playing catch-up in this, but nothing has essentially changed; an agent negotiates a deal and the principles of deal-making remain the same.

There will always be a place for the highly regarded and experienced actor, but for those whose ambitions include becoming a household name or a global brand, that route may soon seem to be too slow and too old-fashioned. When an agent is tasked with designing and developing careers for the next generation of talent, they will be need to be well versed in new technologies and media, and embrace creativity in all formats.

As influencers come out of their niche fields, parlaying their profile and relevancy into a broader landscape, the possibility of these new creatives crossing over into other areas will become not just a distant dream, but a reality. Increasingly, the boundaries between online creative and real-world performer are becoming blurred.

When I talk to creatives about what type of career they would like, they talk about Phoebe Waller-Bridge, they talk about Daniel Evans, they talk about Michaela Coel, they talk about people who work in a number of creative fields and roles, who are unrestrained by the traditional strictures of what can and can't be done, and who evolve their career according to their own evolving interests and abilities. This, I think, is the future for all creatives. These are creatives who lean in to what they love, who work outside of their comfort zone, who are not afraid to get lost in the woods. They are connected with their light-bulb moment, rooted in the need to be part of a tribe, to connect with other people, to tell stories in as many different ways as they can.

Although it is common now to think of the word 'creative' principally as a noun, it has longer been an adjective. It means 'Having the ability or power to create.' Being creative is action. Creativity is a process; it is not a result. Finding a fulfilling creative life goes beyond the limits of landing a West End role, of fame, of fortune, of being a household name. The pandemic made many of us reassess what we need to be creatively fulfilled.

This is where the concept of the multi-platform creative comes in. You may have heard the term 'multi-hyphenate' in the last few years. It's become a very 'zeitgeisty' term. Actually, it's not a new concept. Twenty years ago we would have described someone as having a 'portfolio career'. That term originated in Hollywood in the 1970s, describing a particular type of creative who worked across all fields as a director, producer, writer, designer – not just as an actor. We are seeing an interest in reviving this multi-hyphenate, portfolio, polymath career.

We know that the industry is oversubscribed with actors. There are so many people trying to do it and, by necessity, many are forced to work other jobs. They are realising they would rather their other job was in a creative field of some sort – so they are turning their hand to writing, to directing, or producing, or to any creative field that is complementary to their acting career. They have been served in this by the internet, which has broken down traditional restrictions of physical location and time zones.

As we move forward in the post-pandemic industry, we will discover that some of the old hierarchies and rules of how to be a professional actor have washed away. It's been demonstrated that we can make a living. We can tell stories online. There was so much work produced in so many new formats that it was, at times, dizzying. We got off the path. We got lost in the woods. We presented work that was rough, unfinished, imperfect, incomplete. We set out on our own individual paths. The old industries survived – of course they did – but we learned there was more.

New creatives, content creators and talent in the industry mean that the agents of the future will have to learn how to work across all fields. We will have to step away from the traditional pillars of an actor's career, and work across all media. We need to be unafraid to work in platforms that are not yet fully understood by a lot of the industry – YouTube, TikTok, Snapchat, Instagram, Facebook, Twitter, Clubhouse – and platforms that are yet to be invented…

The new creatives who have come up through those media, building their brand, their profile, and then entering the industry, bring with them new audiences. Those new, young audiences are having their own light-bulb moments and, as they mature, they will change the industry in ways we cannot imagine. The industry will evolve and, to survive and remain relevant, we must evolve with it.

The door has been opened for you. Step through it and embrace all of your creativity, be it writing, directing, producing, casting, making costumes, designing sets, being a graphic designer, writing musicals, writing plays, making films, creating online content, devising streamed concerts, real-world concerts – all of the above.

Whatever you want to do, and however you want to express it, tell your stories. It is how you will survive.

Acknowledgements

Thanks to all my clients, past and present – you have taught me so much about the industry and about creativity.

To all the casting directors – you are the unsung heroes of our industry, not gatekeepers but wise guardians. Thank you to all who contributed thoughts and ideas and quotes.

To Sam and Simon – who took a chance.

Thanks to my husband, Rhys, who read every draft and encouraged me every step.

To Matt Applewhite and the wonderful team at Nick Hern Books – thanks for taking the chance, for correcting my overuse of commas, and for making this better than I imagined it could be. Thank you also for lunch at the Groucho.

To Mum and Dad – who paid. And still pay.

And to Clare O'Toole, the primary-school teacher who started it all off at St Mary's RC Junior in Kilburn – I wish you had lived to see this, I think you would have been proud.